Dollars, Euros, and Debt

*Also by Vito Tanzi*

GOVERNMENT VERSUS MARKET

PUBLIC SPENDING IN THE TWENTIETH CENTURY (*with Ludger Schuknecht*)

INFLATION AND THE PERSONAL INCOME TAX

RECENT CONTRIBUTIONS TO PUBLIC ECONOMICS (*2 volumes*)

# Dollars, Euros, and Debt

## How We Got into the Fiscal Crisis, and How We Get Out of It

Vito Tanzi

palgrave
macmillan

First published 2013 by
PALGRAVE MACMILLAN

Palgrave Macmillan in the UK is an imprint of Macmillan Publishers Limited, registered in England, company number 785998, of Houndmills, Basingstoke, Hampshire RG21 6XS.

Palgrave Macmillan in the US is a division of St Martin's Press LLC, 175 Fifth Avenue, New York, NY 10010.

Palgrave Macmillan is the global academic imprint of the above companies and has companies and representatives throughout the world.

Palgrave® and Macmillan® are registered trademarks in the United States, the United Kingdom, Europe and other countries.

ISBN 978–1–137–34646–9

This book is printed on paper suitable for recycling and made from fully managed and sustained forest sources. Logging, pulping and manufacturing processes are expected to conform to the environmental regulations of the country of origin.

A catalogue record for this book is available from the British Library.

A catalog record for this book is available from the Library of Congress.

# Contents

# Preface and Acknowledgments

During the most significant years when the euro was brought into existence and started operations, I had the privilege of being Director of the Fiscal Affairs Department of the International Monetary Fund, from 1981 until the end of the year 2000, and Undersecretary for Economy and Finance in the Italian government, from 2001 to 2003. In these positions I was in a somewhat privileged position to observe developments, especially in the public finance area, and to follow some of the decisions being taken on some relevant issues.

In the closing months of 2001, when preparations were being made for the introduction of euro bills and coins, to physically replace the national currencies of the members of the European Monetary Union, I chaired a multi-institutional committee, within the Italian government, that addressed some of the logistic problems that would be encountered when, on 1 January 2002, the Italian lira would no longer be the official money of Italy and would be replaced by the euro.

In the months that followed the physical change from the lira to the euro, I often had to meet representatives of consumer groups that, against all the statistical evidence available, kept arguing that the introduction of the euro had led to an enormous increase (a doubling they claimed) in consumer prices, thus making the Italians immediately poorer. Some questioned the exchange rate that had been used in the conversion from the lira to the euro. Others argued that the shops had taken advantage of the change in currency to immediately raise their prices. Still others argued that the introduction of coins, in place of the lira that had used only paper, had increased the weight in the pockets of Italians, forcing them to get rid of their coins more quickly, thus increasing the velocity of that part of the money supply. This relation between weight of money and its velocity was one that had not been theorized by economists!

These and other more or less absurd beliefs were held with great conviction, at times even by economists who should have known better. At the same time some individual members of the Italian government, of which I was part, expressed an embarrassing ambivalence, or, occasionally, even open hostility versus the change that had occurred. The euro had not been welcomed by many groups and by some political forces that had continued to feel nostalgia vis-a-vis the lira and perhaps for the occasional devaluations that it had allowed. In the years that followed, the euro, born under a not-too-welcoming star, would continue to be accused of crimes that it had not committed.

After I left the Italian government, in July 2003, and returned to live in Washington, given my background and professional interests, I continued to follow the fiscal developments in major countries and in Europe and the European Monetary Union and to write articles, for newspapers or for more academic vehicles, on public finance developments in Europe and in the world.

Some of the material in this study was presented, in earlier and much shorter versions: at a seminar, given at the East India Club in London, on 16 April 2012, organized by Politeia, a British think tank located in London. After the seminar, Politeia published a pamphlet based on the lecture, which received useful comments from Dr Sheila Lawlor, the director of Politeia. This book has borrowed some of the ideas first presented in that pamphlet; at the "Consilium 2012" conference, held at the Hyatt Regency Coolum, North of Brisbane (Australia), on 24–25 August 2012, organized by the Centre for Independent Studies, an important Australian think-tank; and at a conference in Sestri Levante (Italy), on 6 October 2012, organized by the Istituto Bruno Leoni, an Italian think-tank. I wish to thank the organizers of these meetings for having given me the incentive to think about some of the issues discussed in this study, and ultimately for having given me the idea of writing this book.

I also wish to thank my son, Alexandre B. Tanzi, an economic reporter for the Bloomberg Network, for numerous discussions on issues related to this study, for helping me with some difficult-to-get data, and for making me aware of articles published by the Bloomberg Network that were relevant for, and used in, parts of this study. Discussions with George Iden, formerly from the IMF, and with Craig Torres, a columnist at Bloomberg News, on some institutional aspects of monetary policy, especially those concerned with monetary unions, were also useful. My thanks go to both of them, while any errors of interpretation remain with me.

Finally, I must express my deep gratitude to my wife, Maria, a former IMF statistician, who, by discussing with me some aspects of payment systems and by, additionally, taking upon herself the full responsibility for running the house, was the perfect companion who created the ideal environment that allowed me to write this book in a short period of time.

*Bethesda, MD* VITO TANZI

# 1
# Introduction

The financial, economic and fiscal crises – the "Great Recession" – that rocked many countries in the years after 2007 have continued to influence the economic developments of several countries, especially but not only in Europe, and, within Europe, in the euro area. In some of their aspects, the crises have generated interesting and at times unexpected reactions on the part of both economists and policy-makers. These unexpected reactions could be interpreted as reflecting intellectual flexibility on the part of some, opportunism on the part of others, and perhaps also continued optimism on the part of others still, with regard to the impact that particular policies can have on economies.

*Discretionary,* or *active,* fiscal policy – to distinguish it from the passive kind associated with the response of truly *automatic,* or *built-in, stabilizers* to economic fluctuations – was quickly resuscitated and promoted, at times with almost religious zeal, by a few vocal and well-placed economists and financial commentators, when the crisis came. Because of the strong criticism that that policy had received, especially during and after the decade of the 1970s (criticism that had earned Nobel prizes for some economists), discretionary fiscal policy had seemed to have lost some, even much, of its attraction, at least among academic economists. However, it had remained popular among politicians and economists working in international institutions, in some think tanks, and in most governments. This would have been obvious to anyone listening during meetings of the Executive Board of the IMF to the interventions of the Fund's executive directors.

At the very beginning of the financial crisis in late 2008, a strong, active fiscal policy, aimed at counteracting the effects of the financial crisis on the economies, had been advocated by some economists, including a number working in international institutions, including the IMF. For example, a paper issued by the IMF on 29 December 2008 had recommended the introduction by countries of an "optimal fiscal package" that should be "timely, large [and] lasting" (see Spilimbergo *et al.*, 2008). However, as time passed, the international institutions became aware of the medium-term consequences that such policies could generate and became more guarded in the statements that they made. They started to worry about the long-run effects of sustained fiscal deficits, in a context of relatively low economic growth, and especially about the consequences of the continuing growth of public debt that was taking place in many countries.

In Europe the impacts of the economic and fiscal crises soon got mixed up in the minds of some observers with the role and the survivability of the euro within the European Monetary Union (EMU), when the so-called "spreads" in interest rates (the differences between the interest rates paid by some countries and the rate paid by Germany) increased sharply and some of the members of the EMU started facing great fiscal difficulties when they saw the cost of their public borrowing rise dramatically, both compared with those of past years and compared with those of countries that at that time were considered fiscally safer. At that point, in the minds of many observers, the problem became the future of the euro, and less that of any specific countries that, especially when the countries were small, would not have attracted so much attention. The so-called *redenomination risk*, the risk associated with the reemergence of national currency – at least for some countries – grew, contributing to the increase in the risk premium that some countries had to pay. This risk influenced the operations of financial operators, including banks.

In this situation, several European countries that were members of the EMU soon discovered the limitations of *discretionary* or *active* fiscal policy, when they faced the unpleasant reality that, if their governments wanted to spend more money to fight the economic downturn than was available to them from their *ordinary* revenue sources, they needed the help of deep-pocketed creditors willing to extend to them the required credit, and at reasonable rates. Alternatively, they would need the proverbial assistance from "rich uncles" (which in principle could be central banks or foreign governments or institutions) willing to provide the additional resources they needed for free or at reasonable rates. It is often forgotten that this reality can be constraining for both individuals and governments, especially when some policy tools, such as the exchange rate and the control over domestic credit expansion, are no longer in the hands of the national authorities, as had become the case for many European countries after they became members of the European Monetary Union and, on 1 January 1999, the eleven participating member states fixed their exchange rates permanently.

Several European countries, and especially those already in precarious fiscal situations before the crisis appeared – which included more countries than is generally believed – were soon faced with *high and rising* interest rates (with higher and growing *spreads vis-à-vis* the countries that were considered safe) on their public borrowing. This occurred in the middle of what, for some other countries, including Germany, the USA, and the UK, might have been considered a credit glut, because of the low rates that the governments of the latter countries needed to pay to borrow money. Interest rates that had diverged little among the EMU countries until 2007 and after around the year 2000, soon diverged significantly, returning to levels similar to those that had existed before the establishment of the eurozone.

In these circumstances, the economic and fiscal crisis, the Great Recession, was seen and experienced by many as a crisis of the euro, and not as a crisis of the individual countries in difficulties. Attention therefore shifted to how to save the euro. This led many observers, especially within the United States and the UK, to ask whether the common currency, which in previous years had been acquiring increasing prominence in the world's economy, and had slowly started to reduce the monopoly power that the dollar had had for decades as the world reserve currency, could survive the economic downturn and the crisis. This shift in emphasis led to a shift of attention towards different policies that presumably could save the euro.

Increasingly the question was asked whether belonging to the EMU, and thus losing the power that national governments generally have to inflate and to devalue their currency, had been a good deal for some of the EMU countries. The credit glut, which had created historically low interest rates for the countries that could benefit from it, was largely the result of the expansionary monetary policies that some central banks had been adopting – policies adopted by the central banks to help some governments deal with the crisis and perhaps also the consequence of excessive saving rates adopted by China and some other countries. Additionally, once the economic crisis started, the reduced borrowing by the private sectors of the countries affected, because of the sharp falls in private investment and in consumption, also contributed to the credit glut in several of the countries considered safe. Before the crisis, China's willingness and ability to buy a large share of the public debt being created by the US government and, to a lesser extent, by some other countries' governments, had also had an impact on the interest rates (and on inflation). This had made the pre-crisis period one of "great moderation," when business cycles had been assumed to have disappeared from our world because of the potency of monetary policy and the wisdom of those who controlled it and when inflation and interest rates had been unusually low.

The policies followed by the central banks in 2008 and in later years sharply increased their balance sheets and helped provide a lot of liquidity to the countries, in the hope that it would help their economies. It also forced other countries to follow similar monetary policies. The low interest rates that the liquidity produced – for some countries – may have also reduced the urgency felt by their governments (especially in the USA, the UK, and also in Japan) to deal more aggressively with their own large fiscal imbalances and their fast-growing public debts. In the short run the burden of a public debt may depend less on its share of GDP, which is the statistic that attracts most attention, than on the cost of financing it, that is on the share of the interest payment in a country's GDP.

On the other hand, the high interest rates paid by the governments of the countries facing borrowing difficulties, several of which were within the European Monetary Union, made it difficult for them to maintain or promote an expansionary use of traditional fiscal policy, as some observers were pushing them, and have continued to push them, to do. The "spreads" between the rates paid by these countries and those paid by the "safe" countries increased dramatically and soon reached very high levels, and, for some countries, levels that were considered unsustainable over the medium run. Therefore, ironically, just when discretionary, expansionary fiscal policy might have seemed, at least to some observers, to be most needed by some countries, it became more difficult for those countries to pursue it, because of the lack of reasonably priced financing.

This was especially the case for several so-called Southern European countries, a group of nations that someone with a sense of humor denominated the PIGS, or, with the addition of Italy, even the PIIGS. Perhaps by coincidence, they were mostly Catholic countries, bringing back in fashion an old sociological theory, that Catholic countries tend to be less virtuous than their Protestant, or Calvinist, counterparts. Similar developments had been observed in several Latin American countries in the 1970s and the 1980s, in the transition economies of East Europe in the 1990s, and in some countries of Southeast Asia during the crisis in 1997–98. The crises in Argentina in 2001–02 and in Mexico in 1995–96 could also be included here.

This study will discuss some of these developments, especially in continental Europe but with frequent references also to the United Kingdom, the United States, or even Japan, which also have been experiencing high fiscal deficits and growing public debts but, so far, without the financing difficulties encountered by the continental European countries. In view of the ongoing debate about the role of fiscal policy during economic crises, the study will go back to the original formulation of the Keynesian fiscal policy, to highlight some of its often forgotten – or ignored – limitations. It will discuss the context in which the fiscal policy was originally formulated, by Keynes and by the early Keynesians, while identifying some of the implicit – but often ignored – assumptions of that policy. Perhaps, it should be mentioned that when we refer to Keynesian policies we do not necessarily refer to the thinking of Keynes himself but to that of the Keynesian school that developed in the late 1930s and the 1940s and that might not always have received Keynes's full endorsement; in some cases Keynes may not have considered himself a true Keynesian.

Some comparisons with the situation prevailing in that other *monetary union* that is the United States of America will also be provided. The reason is that it has been argued, by some well-known and influential economists, that the economic and fiscal problems in the euro area are the direct consequence of a faulty, initial design in the creation of the European Monetary Union, rather than of the misguided fiscal policies that were followed by several of its member countries, especially in the years after the European Monetary Union was created, and that may have had little to do directly with the design of EMU. It will be concluded that the EMU and the USA are much more similar, as monetary unions, than has been assumed. However, the view that the euro's creation was "structurally flawed" may have influenced the behavior of some American hedge fund managers who may have been too quick to take positions that may have lost them or their clients much money.

Although this study is not directly related to the question of whether or not the euro will, or should not, survive, that question will inevitably have some bearing on the discussion. The basic conclusion will be that the problems now affecting several countries, and not just the countries that are members of EMU, have less to do with the initial design of the European Monetary Union and with the role of the euro, although these are likely to have played some role, and a lot more with the *sustainability of the level of public spending* in many of these countries, a level of spending that became increasingly difficult to maintain especially in a world in which financial capital can move freely in and out of a country. We shall, therefore, address the thorny and timely question of what realistic "exit strategies" the countries that are undergoing fiscal crises, and the countries facing potential future crises, could adopt, in order to reduce public spending and to escape from their current or future predicaments.

In the process the study will identify and present what could be called a *fundamental law of the growth of public spending,* a law that may help explain the level reached by the public spending of many countries in recent years. The explicit recognition of this law could play a significant role in developing policies aimed at reducing public spending over the medium and long run. It is always important to identify precisely the origin of a problem in order to deal with it.

The *fundamental law* is a law, or some may prefer to call it a *trend,* that, over the long run, has contributed to the large increase in public spending in many countries. It will be argued that the *increase* in spending has had less of a connection with the welfare programs that were initially introduced in many countries than is generally believed. It will be maintained that recognizing the law and reversing its impact can help with the exit strategies, while to some extent preserving the essence of the welfare states *in their original intentions*. It will be maintained that governments do not need to destroy the welfare systems that were originally established in order to deal with the current crisis. They just need to make the welfare systems more efficient and better focused than they have been, by shedding some of the extra baggage that they have accumulated over the years since their creation. Whether the governments of the countries will be able to make the required reforms remains to be seen. However, in the view of this writer, some of the solutions suggested by various economists and some shortcuts, such as the financing of fiscal deficits by central banks, or, in the case of Europe, the creation of a "fiscal" or "transfer" union, will not bring a solution to the current problems. The solutions must come from the actions of the individual countries, with some potential, time-limited assistance from outside them.

The discussion of the exit strategy will be relevant also for countries that still find it easy to borrow at low rates, but that continue to have high fiscal deficits and growing public debts. These trends will eventually create problems for them, unless they are changed. These countries include Great Britain, the United States, Japan, and some others, where public debts continue to grow at fast rates and fiscal deficits remain high. If not reduced, the current fiscal imbalances of these countries are likely to lead, in future years, to unsustainable high public debts and to serious economic difficulties. It must be recognized that when the health of the patient becomes precarious, surgery may become necessary, and that surgery may possibly, but, one hopes, temporarily, make the patient feel weaker. Thus, the supposedly painless corrections advocated by some economists must be seen with skepticism. Many countries may no longer have the liberty to choose between austerity and growth but all countries have the options of removing structural obstacles to economic growth.

An additional problem to recognize is that, this time around, the level of public debt is high and growing not just in particular, individual countries but also *at the world level*. It is the public debt of the whole world that has gone sharply up, as a share of the world GDP. Furthermore, private debt has also gone up a lot in many countries, creating a strong need for de-leveraging on the part of the whole world. This may create a different reality from that in periods when the high debts were the problems of only some individual countries and some governments. In a world with economies that are much interlinked, through trade or financial relations, the high debts in some countries, and especially in large ones, are likely to have major effects on the economic conditions in others.

For some countries (USA, UK, Japan), the change from the current and apparently comfortable financing situation they are now in to one with growing financing difficulty may not be gradual. History indicates that these changes are often not gradual. As happened in some countries in the past, say Korea and Thailand, in 1997, Mexico in 1982 and 1994, and Argentina in 2001, the change could be sudden and could come when it is not expected. It normally happens if, or when, creditors lose the trust that they have had in lending to countries' governments, while higher private borrowing, and perhaps rising inflationary expectations, begin to affect the nominal interest rate. Therefore, the relatively low inflation and the low interest rates that some of the countries have been enjoying so far (early 2013) should not be interpreted as signaling that their current fiscal policies can continue to be followed in future years; or that these fiscal policies can even be strengthened, as some highly vocal economists have kept arguing, in order to stimulate employment and economic growth. It could simply be the calm before an approaching storm.

Before leaving this introductory section, it should, perhaps, be reiterated that in the view of the author of this study, the current, major economic problem faced by many European countries is not that of the euro, or of how to save the euro. It is the more fundamental one that many of them, and not solely some of those in the European Monetary Union, over the years, have pushed their public spending to levels where it became progressively more difficult to finance it without increasing difficulties and without encountering major resistance either from taxpayers or from potential creditors. Without reducing the levels of public spending that have created difficulties, levels that may not be the same for different countries, because of different reactions to taxes, the countries of the EMU and of some other countries (including US, UK, and Japan) will not be spared the fiscal crisis that, so far, has focused the attention of many economists on the EMU and on the euro.

Fiscal crises are always more difficult to solve than financial crises, because they involve the role of many politicians and affect more citizens. The time may have come for basic surgery. Dealing with symptoms may no longer be sufficient. Of course this does not mean that the behavior of banks and other agents in the financial sector has not played an important role. Financial liberalization has made it possible for some banks in some countries to make bad investments and at a level that would not have been possible when capital flows across countries were better controlled. This has clearly been the problem with the banks of Cyprus and of some other countries. In several cases the loans were provided to finance large public spending.

Finally let us imagine what might have happened if the European Monetary Union had not been there and every EMU country had attempted to deal with the financial crisis that hit all the countries with monetary expansion and with increased public spending. Are we sure that the results would have been better as some observers seem to imply? Are we sure that competitive devaluations and inflationary finance of fiscal deficits would not have followed? The euro may have imposed some coordination and discipline that would not have been possible without it.

# 2
# The Crisis and the Calls for Policy Responses

We shall start with a discussion of whether Keynesian fiscal policy can still be used to promote an economic expansion in the countries in crisis, given the precarious fiscal situation of many of those that are still experiencing high unemployment, economic slowdown, or even recessions. The use of *discretionary*, or *active*, fiscal policy, to counter the economic and social effects of recessions, as proposed by Lord Keynes three-quarters of a century ago, has been widely debated, especially since the start of the Great Recession in 2008. Some of the participants in the debate – which has involved economists, policymakers, civil servants, financial operators, reporters, union leaders, and even normal citizens – advocated, and have continued to advocate, a relaxed fiscal stance, one that in their view would maintain or even increase, in the short run, the high fiscal deficits that many countries have been experiencing. These individuals have continued to argue that such a fiscal policy (which would require higher fiscal deficits) would help sustain a higher aggregate demand (as Keynes had theorized, during the "Great Depression" of the 1930s). They see the current economic difficulties of countries mainly in terms of lack of sufficient aggregate demand, in spite of very high current fiscal deficits that for sure must be contributing to aggregate demand. The high fiscal deficits are too high to be attributed to the falls in the countries' GDPs. Higher fiscal deficits would, presumably, increase the aggregate demands of the countries, thus contributing to higher employment and greater economic activity, and promoting a faster economic growth. This, in their view, would contribute to a reduction in the fiscal deficit as a share of GDP over the medium run by making GDP grow, or grow at a faster rate. However, by increasing demand, a short-run expansion might be obtained, but not growth, which is a longer-run phenomenon.

Some of these commentators have lamented that the "fiscal stimulus packages" enacted by the governments of many countries, including the United States, in the early years of the financial crisis, had not been large enough to do the required job. In their view, the medicine had been the right one but the dosage had been insufficient. Others have complained that, regardless of their sizes, when they were introduced, the fiscal stimulus packages had not been maintained long enough. The governments had started talking too soon about reducing the fiscal deficits, or introducing measures aimed at this. Some observers have continued to push for a continuation of, or even for increasing, the high fiscal deficits, until unemployment and economic growth return to pre-recession, or "normal," levels.

It should be noted that in these discussions the pre-recession growth rate of the economy has been considered "normal," rather than "bubble-inflated." The above-mentioned observers argue that "growth" should be the objective of current fiscal policy and not "austerity," and that growth requires a more relaxed and more expansionary fiscal policy. These observers have had no doubts that higher fiscal deficits would be the medicine needed to restore good health to the sick economies, as Keynes had theorized. The debate has been about the dosage and the length of use of the medicine, not about whether the medicine might have been the wrong one, given the conditions of the patients.

The most outspoken and visible proponent of these views has undoubtedly been Paul Krugman, a professor of economics at Princeton University, who received the Nobel prize in economics for his research on why nations with similar endowments trade among themselves. He writes a regular and widely read column in the *New York Times*. His high professional status and the visibility of his column have given his views wide circulation and influence. He has used his column, as well as some recent popular books that he has written, to continue arguing for more fiscal expansion, especially in the United States, but also in Europe. He does not seem at all concerned about the precarious fiscal situation of both areas, believing that a fiscal expansion especially if directed to investment in infrastructures and other growth-promoting areas will make the economies grow faster, which will help solve the fiscal problem by reducing the ratio of public debt to GDP. He has also shown impatience toward views that are contrary to his.

The views of Paul Krugman have been endorsed, or shared to considerable extent, at least in the United States, by some other well-known economists, including Larry Summers and Christina Romer, both of whom played important roles in the first two years of the Obama administration, at the time when the US fiscal stimulus package was introduced (see Suskind, 2011), and by some well-placed economic commentators, especially in Europe, who have also been pushing for expansionary fiscal policy in European countries.

The politicians of several of the countries in difficulty have complained about the austerity measures that lack of debt financing, obtainable at reasonable rates, was forcing them to adopt for their countries. In this attitude, they have been strongly supported by the leaders of the countries' labor unions, who have opposed almost any measures that would have reduced acquired benefits for workers and pensioners. Several economists have also complained that what they called austerity was contributing to depressing the economies and making it more difficult for the countries to get out of their depressed states.

Austerity is never popular with the public, especially when several policymakers have become convinced that its pursuit inevitably reduces economic activity and the welfare of the citizens, as it often does for some countries, in the short run. It is also not popular with convinced Keynesians who believe that there is often a way out of it, through expansionary policies. Many citizens do not understand the reasons for the austerity measures, especially when they hit their wallets. In several countries, attempts at reducing public spending, often bring street demonstrations that at times turn violent. The threat or the occurrence of these demonstrations inevitably makes politicians less willing to push for policies that would reduce the existing benefits for the citizens, even when they consider that these measures are necessary from a macroeconomic or a fiscal-sustainability point of view.

On the other hand, other economists and observers and some policymakers have worried about the sharp rise in the interest rates that the borrowing governments of several European countries have had to pay in recent years to get loans, and about the fast growth in public debts experienced by European and some other countries. In some non-continental-European countries, the public debt share of GDP is increasing in spite of the fact that these countries are still benefiting from very low borrowing rates, and from seigniorage payments made by central banks that depend on the profits that the central banks make on their monetary actions.

By sharply reducing interest payments, low interest rates have reduced the measured fiscal imbalances of countries such as the United States, the United Kingdom and Japan below what they would have been for these countries, had they been paying the rates that they paid in normal times in the past. For example, the interest cost on the very high US public debt in 2011 was 3.1 percent of GDP while it was 4.8 percent of GDP in 1991 when the public debt was a much lower share of GDP. Or, assume that the USA paid, today, the same interest rates as Spain or Italy. An increase in the low interest rates could quickly lead to sharp increases in the fiscal deficits of these countries. This happened in the past in several countries, including the USA, in the early 1980s. The sharp and rapid increase in interest rates and not the level of the public debt was also the main factor that led to the Argentine sovereign debt default in 2001–02 (see Tanzi, 2007a).

An obvious explanation for the low rates paid by some countries is the expansionary monetary policy of their central banks, combined with the fact that, compared with the difficulties faced by some of the European countries that are members of EMU, and that no longer have independent *national* central banks that can provide credit to their governments, they are seen as still relatively "safe countries" in which institutions and individuals with excess balances, from all countries, can invest their money. The Chinese buying of US public securities has clearly helped to keep the rates down. In other words, at least for the time being, some countries continue to be seen as "safe havens" for people and institutions with excess balances to invest their money. Some commentators have gone as far as to maintain that countries that have a national bank can never experience sovereign debt default because, presumably, their central banks can print money to service their debts. This of course assumes that all the debts of these countries are in their domestic currencies, currencies that can be produced at (almost) zero cost and without limit by a country's national bank and that those who lend money to the governments will continue to do so while the debt is being liquidized by inflation – which in the absence of hyperinflation could take a long time.

Many economists and financial operators, however, now worry about the medium- and long-run *sustainability* of current fiscal policies in several countries, and not just European ones, especially when it is assumed that the current fiscal imbalances are to be maintained in the future and when they are combined with the impact on public spending that will be coming from existing entitlement programs and ongoing demographic trends. These worries inevitably can carry with them some stock adjustments, to transfer balances from countries seen to be in danger to safer ones. To some extent this is what has happened in Europe where German and other countries' investments in Greece have been liquidated, contributing to the Greek problems.

The entitlement programs that exist in many countries have created kinds of "property rights" for the countries' citizens against their own states. The fact that many experts believe that the rates of economic growth in many countries are likely to remain low in future years – because of low investments in recent years, no new economically significant technologies on the horizon, shrinking labor forces, and precarious financial conditions – make the current fiscal policies of many countries clearly unsustainable, unless they are significantly changed. Theories or models of (long-term) growth have never included fiscal deficits or public debt levels as determinants of growth.

The enormous future liabilities created by existing social legislation, combined with demographic trends that are without doubt fiscally and economically unfriendly – because they increase the ratio of retirees to workers and increase health costs for the retirees – would make the public spending of many countries grow at high rates, in future years, rates that could lead to fiscal crises even in the countries that are now seen as safe. Given this situation, it would be highly imprudent to keep adding new liabilities to the anticipated ones, as some economists would like to do, unless there were a certainty, or at least a high probability, that the additional spending would be highly productive in terms of economic growth, thus raising the denominator in the debt/GDP ratio. However it may be optimistic, or even naive, to assume this scenario in democratic countries, where decisions on spending are made by politicians and not by apolitical experts. It is not likely that the higher spending would go to highly productive investments, and in short enough time, to make a difference to the growth rate before it makes the share of the debt to GDP rise.

The above describes the situation of the United States, where economists, such as Larry Kotlikoff, Jagadeesh Gokhale and some others, have been worrying about the enormous difference that now exists in that country between the net, present (discounted) value of future federal government liabilities, created by the entitlement programs now in force, and the present (discounted) value of future federal revenue, derived from current tax laws. Kotlikoff has estimated the present value of this current "fiscal gap" in the USA to be of the order of $222 trillion (*sic*). This is an extraordinary figure that, to be reduced, will require major and painful structural reforms in the years to come. Gokhale has estimated that the fiscal imbalance "amounts to 5.4 percent of the present value of future U.S. gross domestic product, or 11.7 percent of the present value of future payrolls" (Gokhale, 2013, p. 2). The fiscal gap reported above make the current US fiscal situation clearly unsustainable over the long run, without major reforms. And the longer the reforms are delayed the greater the fiscal gap will become.

It would require enormous and potentially unsustainable increases in the ratio of taxes to GDP in future years to eliminate the fiscal gap from the revenue side. A slowing down of future growth below the one assumed in the estimates would raise the above figure. The "fiscal cliff" faced on 1 January 2013, that is forcing some fiscal adjustment on the US government, worried some observers that feared that the adjustment, might occur too rapidly and might plunge the country into a recession. However there was no particular, negative reaction by the market to the forced reduction in public spending. On the contrary the stock market reacted positively. More adjustment is still needed and must take place at some not too distant time. The USA may have the "advantage" of having a tax burden that is still relatively low, compared with that of European countries. For example, it still does not have a value added tax. So, in principle, there is more scope for a potential adjustment coming from the revenue side. However, in the US there seems to be more resistance from taxpayers than in Europe, to paying higher taxes and the politics of tax increases may be more complex.

The situation of several other countries is equally worrisome and in many of them tax increases are objectively more difficult than in the USA because of their already high levels. Only major reforms, and especially those aimed at reducing public spending, combined with structural reforms that increase growth, can make their fiscal situation sustainable. It is an illusion to believe that a fiscal expansion, pursued under current fiscal circumstances, would change this reality. A fiscal expansion that required more government spending might simply add to the future expenditure cuts or to the tax increases that will become necessary.

It should be added that an expectation of future tax increases cannot be counted on to contribute much to the reduction in the fiscal imbalances, because of more intense political resistance to higher taxes in recent years in many countries, and because of the growing globalization of economic activities that have created what the author of this book has in other writings called "fiscal termites" (see Tanzi, 2001). Fiscal termites are political and especially administrative impediments to higher tax rates that have been making it increasingly more difficult for countries to adopt higher tax rates, and to raise tax revenue. The globalization of economic activities, the increasing exchanges of non-tangible products between countries, including the exchange of trademarks and use of patents, and purchases through the use of the internet, are examples of the impact that new technologies are having on tax systems and on the ability to raise tax levels. These new technologies have contributed over the years to the rise in importance of fiscal termites.

Tax evasion at the international level has been growing over the years, as recent newspaper stories and various studies have made evident. See, *inter alia*, Brooks, 2012. This has become a major problem for many countries, including the United States, in spite of national and international efforts to fight it. The number of tax havens has remained high. This means that the solution to the fiscal imbalances of many countries is not likely to come from the tax side. Of course, *some* tax increases may seem possible, at least from a comparative point of view, especially in countries where the levels of taxation are still relatively low compared with other countries, as would seem to be the case in the United States and Japan. However, in these countries strong and growing political resistance to higher taxes has been evident over the years. This resistance is likely to reduce the scope for significant tax increases. For example, as mentioned, the USA still does not have a value added tax; and in Japan the rate for that tax has remained remarkably low in spite of the fast-growing public debt and the high fiscal deficits that the country has experienced over many years. That situation is not likely to change much. The recent French and Italian governments that have tried to improve the fiscal situation with tax increases have encountered major resistance and sharp criticism and, in Italy, Mario Monti has experienced an embarrassing election loss partly for his attempt to raise taxes.

For the OECD countries as a group, the highest tax levels were reached *before, or by, the year 2000,* with a couple of exceptions (Portugal and Spain). These latter countries, before the Great Recession, had benefited from the higher revenue generated by the bubbles, especially the bubbles in the housing sector (see Tanzi, 2012b). Between the years when the share of taxes into GDP reached the highest levels for OECD countries (often in the 1990s) and the year 2008, the year when the sub-prime crisis appeared, *all* OECD countries, with the single and trivial exception of Italy, where taxes had increased a little, had experienced significant *reductions* in the shares of taxes into GDPs (see Tanzi, 2011a, table 4.1, on p. 95, and table 4.3, on p. 104). These tax reductions, which in some cases were large (8 percent of GDP in Ireland, around 6 percent of GDP in the Netherlands and Sweden, and above 4 percent of GDP in Canada, Australia, New Zealand, Finland, and Luxembourg), were in part due to the increasing taxpayers' resistance to high taxes and to the growing technical or administrative difficulties in increasing tax revenue, in an environment that was becoming more globally integrated and in which the effect of the fiscal termites mentioned earlier was being increasingly felt.

In conclusion, it would be an illusion to expect that tax increases will play a major role in future years in correcting the countries' fiscal imbalances. The major part of the needed adjustment will have to come from expenditure reductions unless the miracle of fast growth took place. How quickly this adjustment in public spending should be made has much to do with the ongoing debate among experts. However, the longer is the delay, the greater will be the adjustment that becomes necessary.

Some economists have advocated fiscal restraint and structural policies that would, over a reasonable period, significantly reduce both public spending and fiscal deficits, while, at the same time, attempting to increase economic growth through structural reforms that do not require additional public spending. This might be possible by removing supply-side obstacles to growth that continue to exist in most countries. Many of these have to do with impediments to the free use of labor and with tax laws that at times penalize the use of both labor and capital. Pushes for "right to work laws" have acquired some energy in some countries and may help remove some obstacles.

A few economists, including Alberto Alesina at Harvard, have questioned, or downplayed, the argument, made by those who want to maintain or increase the current fiscal deficits, about the assumed negative impact that lowering public spending would have on aggregate demand and on economic growth. This potentially negative impact has been a policy scarecrow in some countries, deterring some policymakers from proposing changes that could be beneficial to fiscal balances, if not immediately then at least in the medium run.

These economists have pointed to the examples of countries that in past years had reduced, at times by significant amounts, their public spending without suffering the negative consequences that the fiscal expansionists had predicted, and continue to predict, when these reductions are made. There is evidence of several countries that did very well in the years after they cut the spending by significant amounts but paired those cuts with other growth-promoting reforms. (See various papers, over the years, by Alesina and Ardagna, especially 2010, and by Schuknecht and Tanzi, especially 2005; see also Tanzi, 2011a.)

Worried about their precarious or deteriorating fiscal situations, several of the European countries (including those in immediate difficulties, also UK and to a lesser extent Italy) recently started to take some actions; others have promised to take action aimed at bringing their fiscal accounts under better controls. These restrictive policies continue to be criticized by some economists. (See, for example, various papers at Vox, an economic website, and Corsetti, 2012.) However, it could be argued that in several countries the actions are still relatively timid and the deficit-reducing policies have, in some cases and in the short run, been based more on attempts to raise tax revenue (as in Italy and France) than on significant cuts in public spending.

Street demonstrations and, often, strong political opposition by members of labor unions and other interest groups, such as pensioners, that do not understand, or do not wish to understand, the dangers of unchanged current spending policies, or who have strong vested interests in the continuation of those policies, have made it difficult for governments to cut their public spending significantly. Also, strong beliefs in the existence of Keynesian solutions, or in "Keynesian" or "monetarist" free lunches, have made some governments still hopeful that there is a realistic and comfortable choice between a growth-based, and Keynesian-fueled, strategy, and one based on sustainable reductions in public spending combined with structural reforms.

The latest *Fiscal Monitor* (April 2013), a useful, bi-annual report on fiscal developments, prepared by the IMF, indicates that some reductions in the shares of public spending into GDP can be expected in future years, especially in the countries undergoing major difficulties, such as Greece, Iceland, Ireland, Portugal, Spain, and also the UK, and to a lesser extent in Italy. However, public spending may still remain too high in some of these countries. At this stage (early 2013) nobody knows what will happen in the United States and in Japan. In Japan there is even talk of a new fiscal stimulus package. In some of the above countries, part of the reduction may be due to the end of public support for the private banks or for the bubble sectors that existed in earlier years. In several of the OECD countries the expected reduction in public debt is modest while in some – US, UK, Japan, and Spain – the share of public debt into GDP is expected to keep going up in the next few years. In Italy it went sharply up in 2012 in spite of the measures introduced by the Monti government.

It should be repeated that often the major economic problem, at least in the short run, is not so much the ratio of the public debt to GDP, a ratio that attracts much or all of the attention but the cost of servicing the debt as a share of GDP. For example the low cost of servicing the public debt has allowed the Japanese economy to go on with a huge and rising debt/GDP ratio without experiencing, so far, an economic disaster. The question is: how much longer can this go on? Should the financing costs of the debt increase significantly in future years, Japan and similar countries could encounter quick and major problems. The financing costs may not increase if the growth rates of the economies remain low, a development which could also lead to major fiscal problems. This could become a problem especially for Japan, the United States, and the UK, which, in spite of their high debts, continue to pay low shares of GDPs in interest payments, but which have now low growth rates. In Greece much of the recent international assistance has been directed at reducing the cost of the debt, although it is the share of the debt into GDP, which is lower than in Japan, that has continued to attract the attention of commentators.

Uncertainty remains also as to whether the current fiscal restraints that some governments are trying to introduce in some of the countries would be sustained by future governments. This uncertainty is likely to help keep the spreads from coming down significantly, for some time and in some countries, after some measures to reduce the fiscal deficit have been introduced. This might be a problem at this time (early 2013) in Italy, even though the spread over Germany has fallen, because some of the reforms that had been introduced by the Monti government might be undone by future governments, made up as they might be of political elements that had been critical of the economic policies of the Monti government. For political, ideological, or simply opportunistic reasons, future governments might be tempted to reverse the policies that had aimed at reducing public spending. This possibility has obvious implications for current and future interest rates.

This uncertainty about the future increases the *value of waiting*, in making investments or hiring decisions, for some or many private investors, who may have the financial means to invest but are reluctant to take the decisions while significant uncertainty remains. At least in some countries, and especially in the United States, the major problem for enterprises has not been lack of funds, which they seem to have had in abundance, but lack of incentives to invest. In some countries the uncertainty about the future may encourage capital flight. Indeed capital flight has been a major problem in some European countries, including Greece, Italy, Cyprus, and some others. Later we argue that even in the absence of capital flight the lack of incentive to invest may be influenced by concerns about the fiscal situation.

# 3
# Central Banks as Lenders of Last Resort

There have been strong pressures on the European Central Bank to play the role of the traditional, rich and generous uncle, for some of the countries that use the euro. Many observers have been urging the ECB to buy, directly, from the issuing governments, or indirectly, through the secondary market, the bonds of the governments of the countries in difficulty. It has been argued that this action would keep the spreads low, without leading to inflation, because of the high unemployment and excess capacity that exists in those economies. It has also been argued that the spreads may not be justified because they are the result of irrational confidence crises fed by some "herd behavior" on the part of holders of government bonds. Some other observers, and especially Hans-Werner Sinn, a German economist, in several recent papers, have argued that so-called TARGET2 balances have indirectly allowed huge funds to work their ways to countries in difficulties, and especially to Greece, thus reducing the need for these countries to adjust. We shall discuss later, in another chapter, this complex issue that has attracted much debate, especially in 2012.

The ECB is not allowed by its constitution to buy government bonds *directly* from the issuing governments and it cannot bail out governments in difficulties. Its goal is, *legally,* supposed to be that of maintaining stable prices, a restriction that had originally been imposed by the Germans owing to their historic fear of inflation. However, with the approval of its governing body, made up of the representatives of the national central banks, it can buy government bonds from the secondary market, if this action is seen to keep the interest rates, that national governments pay for borrowing, from rising excessively. It has been doing this on a substantial scale.

In the summer of 2012, the president of the European Central Bank, Mario Draghi, announced that the Bank was prepared to buy government bonds on a scale large enough to protect the euro, a statement that helped calm the market, thus reducing the spreads for several countries. However, Draghi declared that the ECB would do so while requesting that the countries made what he considered needed structural reforms, including those to make the welfare states less expensive. Thus, he introduced an element of *conditionality* in this important and unlimited commitment by the European Central Bank to help countries in financial difficulty and, especially, to save the euro.

This commitment by the ECB would facilitate the servicing of their public debts by governments while giving responsible countries some incentive and more time to make needed and agreed reforms. However, a danger is also that it might allow some less responsible or less courageous governments to delay the introduction of deficit-reducing measures, because it would reduce the pressure on governments to make the needed fiscal adjustments soon, and that it might also allow some investors to dispose of the bonds in their possession and take their capital out of the countries in which they had been invested. This potential "moral hazard" problem became evident in some countries in 2011 and 2012 when the ECB started buying government bonds and some governments relaxed their pursuit of needed reforms while some investors may have taken the opportunity to disinvest in some countries. These problems obviously cannot be ignored by the ECB.

This bond-buying policy has been followed, on a substantial scale, also by the US Federal Reserve Bank, which, unlike the ECB, has the more ambitious and flexible mandate of balancing price stability against promoting "maximum employment." The mandate of the ECB is narrower, being limited to the promotion of price stability, which, in principle, should prevent it from engaging in monetary policy to promote other objectives, unless it can justify it on the ground of promoting "financial stability." The pursuit of these other objectives, if continued, might, sooner or later, lead to inflation and to other problems, taking monetary policy away from its narrower and traditional goals.

The Federal Reserve Bank, even more than the ECB, has pursued unorthodox policies that, in the view of some observers, have, to some extent, transformed monetary policy into fiscal policy. In the short period between November 2008 and March 2009, it bought $1750 billion of US Treasury bonds and assets of private banks, while it also made large amounts of dollar reserves available to foreign central banks. Also, "[b]etween December 2007 and March 2010, [it] auctioned a total of $3.81 trillion, collateralised funds, with maturities of 28 or 84 days" (see Puddu and Walchli, 2012, p. 1) These authors have argued that the banks that received these Fed loans had "adopted a riskier strategy with short-term debt, higher leverage and high asset risks," compared with the banks that did not receive Fed loans, and that the Fed, through the Term Auction Facility (TAF) program, had acted as a lender of last resort to banks. They conclude that the program had amounted to "countercyclical policy," not through the use of fiscal instruments but with that of monetary instruments.

More recently the Federal Reserve Bank has followed with other expansionary and increasingly controversial actions. So-called "quantitative easing" (QE) policies, of which there have been, so far, three phases – I, II, and III – have injected, and, it has been promised, will to continue to inject, large amounts of liquidity into the American (and world) economy, in the hope that by lowering even more the already exceptionally low interest rates, such actions would help promote an economic recovery and contribute to "maximum employment." In December 2012, the Fed announced that it would maintain interest rates at their very low level until the unemployment rate in the US fell to 6.5 percent. The assumption was that, as long as the unemployment rate remains above 6.5 percent, there would not be a danger of inflation. Thus investors can make investments under the certainty that for a long while the Fed will continue with the low rates. One can only hope that the assumption about the lack of inflationary effect proves to be a correct one and that the policy does not lead to significant bubbles and related problems. The Bank of England has followed broadly similar policies by buying large amounts of government bonds and other assets from the market.

Therefore, even in the absence of "global warming," the world is being inundated with vast amounts of liquidity created by central banks. The Fed's balance sheet could reach four trillion dollars in

2013 if current policies are continued for the rest of the year. So far these injections of liquidity, which have remained highly controversial, do not seem to have made much noticeable, positive impact on either employment or economic activities. But then it is difficult to tell what would have happened without such policies. At the same time, the policies have raised growing skepticism and concerns about their longer-term effects, on the part of many observers, including many financial market operators. These reactions must inevitably have some impact on the willingness of investors to tie their financial assets into real investments. Of course there are also observers that have approved and endorsed these actions by the central banks, and representatives of the central banks have generally, with some dissenting voices, defended them (see Blinder, 2012).

A concern on the part of some observers is that, by artificially lowering both short-term and long-term interest rates, these policies inevitably change the allocation of resources made by the market and are likely to contribute to creating new asset bubbles, in the stock and bond market, in the commodity markets, and possibly in other areas. This had happened in the years before 2008, contributing to the sub-prime financial crisis. Because of the growing uncertainty about the more distant future the low interest policies may lead to preferences for short-term investments of which the investors can more easily divest themselves. Sooner or later the bubbles could lead to inflationary problems, as economic theory suggests and as some economists are predicting; see, for example, Martin Feldstein's column in the *Financial Times* of 28 September 2012.

In the United States the Fed's monetary policy has definitely contributed to making the fiscal outcome for that country *look* significantly better than it would have otherwise looked, and not because of a pickup in economic activity. This may have had an impact on policy decisions. It looks better because low interest rates have kept the cost of financing the large and growing US public debt low, while they have provided the government with higher seigniorage revenue from the central bank than otherwise would have been the case. As mentioned, those actions are likely to create major distortions in the allocation of resources in the market and probably lead to long-run lower growth rates for the economy.

Given the current enormous size of the US public debt, the reduction in the cost of its public debt can easily amount to several percentage points of GDP. As A. Gary Shilling put it, in a recent Bloomberg's column (30 October 2012):

> I wouldn't suggest... that these low financing costs encourage Congress and the administration to delay dealing with the mushrooming federal debt. Still, after deducting its own operating expenses, the Fed returns the interest it receives on the holding of Treasuries and agency securities to the Treasury, helping to offset the deficit... [I]n the past three years the Fed has remitted $200 billion to the Treasury.

In his column Shilling also discussed various other distortions in the market connected with the extremely low interest rates, including the issuance by some institutions of bonds that do not mature for 100 years and the fact that "interest rates close to zero have made highly leveraged speculation in commodities very cheap."

A recent study by the IMF (see IMF, 2012b), after pointing out that since the start of the financial crisis the balance sheets of central banks have expanded enormously and that, between 2007 and 2011, the liabilities of the ECB doubled in size, while those of the Fed and the Bank of England more than tripled, concluded that these expansions provided significant short-run benefits to the public finances of these countries. Since 2008 the seigniorage, generated *per year,* in selected advanced countries by quantitative easing policies was estimated at over 2 percent of GDP. This is indeed a large amount. These short-run benefits will present problems in the future if potential losses "incurred by the central bank on... asset holdings... create a need for capital injection from the government to recapitalize the central bank" (see ibid., p. 18). A recent study by well-known monetary economists and Fed observers has worried about "an adverse feedback loop in which doubts by lenders [could] lead to higher sovereign interest rates which in turn make the debt problems more severe [for high debt countries]." That study has also simulated the possibility of substantial Fed's net losses 4–5 years from now (see Greenlaw *et al.*, 2013).

The promoters of these policies and their defenders stress that *so far* there has been relatively little pressure on prices and believe that the central banks would be able to prevent inflationary pressures from getting out of hand, if inflation appeared to become an imminent danger. However, we have little knowledge of how long are the lags between the time when monetary expansion takes place and that when the positive, or the negative, effects of the expansion on employment, prices, and bubbles become clearly visible. So far there has been relatively little evidence of both of these effects. However, it was the existence of these lags that often confused policymakers in the past, including the Fed chairman Alan Greenspan, before 2007, and that led to the financial crisis. Historical experience indicates that by the time price pressures become evident, it may often be too late to deal effectively with the problems they create. How much evidence does the Fed have to guarantee that an unemployment rate of more than 6.5 percent guarantees that no inflationary forces will be set in motion by its low interest rates policy?

Large increases in liquidity created by central banks' policies usually lead to the devaluation of the currencies of the countries that engage in them and in time encourage other countries to pursue similar policies. It may be no coincidence that the trade balance of the United States improved recently when its exchange rate lost some value. If the countries that engage in these policies are economically important, as is obviously the case for the US, the devaluation of their currency also leads to complaints from other countries about currency manipulation and about the impact on other countries' exchange rates, thus potentially inviting retaliations on the part of these countries. If continued, these policies could even lead eventually to "currency wars," should countries such as China, Brazil, Australia, and others retaliate. There have been growing complaints from the policy-makers of several countries about the monetary policy followed by the USA.

The bottom line is that active monetary policies, such as quantitative easing and similar policies, distort the *domestic* and *world* allocation of resources that would have existed without those policies, thus potentially affecting future economic performances. They also affect the harmonious relations that should exist among the policymakers of the world's major economies. The role that the G-20 had been expected to play at the beginning of the financial crisis seems to have become less ambitious and less visible than had been originally expected. Global policy coordination reached its highest level in the G-20 London Summit of April 2009. Since then cooperation has been less evident. The G7 meeting of 12 February 2013 in Moscow felt the need to reaffirm in its declaration the "longstanding commitment to market determined exchange rates..." and that the countries "will not target exchange rates." Several observers including Pascal Lamy, the head of the WTO, have expressed concern about growing protectionism.

What seems plausible and consistent with basic economic theory is that the injection of all this liquidity may *sooner or later* have *some* economic consequences, and these consequences may not necessarily be the ones desired by those who advocate the policies: namely increasing employment and economic activity, without inflation and with sustained higher economic growth, in spite of the distortions that are being created. Of more direct immediate consequence to fiscal policy is that the injection of a lot of liquidity, especially liquidity connected with the buying of public bonds, may create moral hazard problems, by reducing the pressures on some governments to take corrective actions on the fiscal front. For example, in the USA there has been so far little movement toward seriously dealing with its long-run fiscal problem and not just with the fiscal cliff that has attracted most of the attention of the media. In the USA any adjustment has been left, so far, to a discussion about what to do about the mechanical impact of the fiscal cliff that is, in some sense, an indication of the absence of responsible policy action. It had been feared, by some, that by reducing, mechanically, the fiscal deficit by a significant amount, the fiscal cliff could plunge the American economy back into a recession. It is of course also possible that the fiscal cliff could have beneficial non-Keynesian effects, by reducing the US fiscal imbalance.

As noted earlier, in some European countries, there was a noticeable slowdown in the introduction of structural reforms in 2011–12, when the ECB accelerated its bond-buying policy. And the Japanese authorities have continued to postpone any needed fiscal adjustment while its public debt has continued to move toward the stratosphere. The new Japanese government in 2013 intends to experiment again with fiscal "stimulus packages" and with monetary extension. These stimulus packages in the late 1990s did not seem to have had the intended effect but helped create the current fiscal mess (see Tanzi, 2008b, pp. 122–5).

The direct purchase of government bonds from governments used to be called "inflationary finance" in the past. Given the bad experiences with the use of this policy, in Latin American, East European and other countries, including Germany after World War One, inflationary finance had been largely banned, as a desired policy tool, from economic discussion and from the economic textbooks, and especially from use by countries. The campaign for the independence of central banks that had been conducted vigorously by the economic profession in the past two decades, and that, until recently, had seemed to have been successful and had led to low inflation, had had much to do with the danger that central banks might be used politically by governments. This danger had been common in Latin American countries, and also in some other countries including Italy up to the 1980s until the so-called "divorce" between the Italian central bank and the Italian Treasury. In those situations central banks became agents of fiscal policy, replacing, to some extent, taxes with money creation, in the financing of public spending (see Tanzi, 1978).

It is worrisome that the independence of central banks has started to be seen by some as a handicap rather than as an asset, implying that politics should play a larger role in the central banks' decisions. (See, for a recent example, the comment by Peter Tasker in the *Financial Times* of 12 January 2013.) If one believes in the existence of liquidity traps, one may also believe that in some occasions taxes could be replaced by direct money creation by central banks. Some of the earliest Keynesians, including Abba Lerner, had believed in this possibility. Inflationary finance may be, politically, for the policymakers of some countries, an easier policy to follow than tax increases in order to finance public spending, especially when the public spending can be justified by uses such as to build infrastructure which can be claimed that they stimulate growth. If spending is considered a prerequisite for the growth of the economy, as some seem to believe at this time on both sides of the Atlantic, then inflationary finance may be promoted as a reasonable and convenient policy, especially until inflation appears. To some extent the push for engaging in the building of infrastructures at this time, taking advantage of cheap interest rates financed indirectly by central banks, is a return to "inflationary finance," but so far an "inflationary finance" without inflation. A large investment program in infrastructure in Japan in the second half of the 1990s did not generate the expected results (see Tanzi, 2008b, ch. 6, especially pp. 122–6). Now the call is to replace the unproductive and "aging" infrastructure of the 1990s with new infrastructure, as suggested by Tasker.

Over recent years, the independence that the central banks had gained had led to a world with lower inflation than in the past, at least since the end of the gold standard. This may change in future years, unless permanently depressed economies lead to permanent changes in the nature of some economic relationships, by creating what seem to be *permanent liquidity traps,* as some believe may have happened in Japan. However, in economics there may be nothing that is permanent. There are often arguments that sound superficially good and that can be advanced, and are being advanced today, by some economists, to justify expansionary monetary and also expansionary fiscal policies, at least in the short run. Some of these arguments were also occasionally made in the past, in other places and other contests (see Tanzi, 1978). The current arguments aim at convincing listeners that "this time is different" or, what may be the same, that "this time the conditions are different and that those who make the policy decisions are smarter than those who made past decisions." However, generally, *but with uncertain lags and timing,* the expected economic relationships that the theory predicts tend to reestablish their primacy.

Using the argument that "this time is different," or, alternatively, that when a house is on fire it is not the time to worry about the moral hazard that may be created by having access to firemen, some economists and commentators have advocated the direct purchase of government bonds by the central banks and, especially, by the ECB, downplaying the lessons from the past, or minimizing the likely inflationary consequences, that may emerge at some point, in the medium and longer run, were such a policy followed. These proponents argue that this action, which would make the ECB the lender of last resort, *not to banks, for which it has always been a legitimate role, but to governments,* would keep the interest rates paid by the governments low, by preventing speculative spirals that, in their view, do not reflect the real fiscal situations of governments, but can damage their creditworthiness.

This direct lending by the central bank would presumably give the countries time to adjust their fiscal accounts while keeping the spreads down and thus save the euro. (See, especially, various papers by Paul De Grauwe.) All this would happen without creating: inflationary pressures for the countries; moral hazards on the part of policymakers; or major distortions in the allocation of resources.

This policy would, it is argued, help rescue the euro from its current difficulties, and would be a cheap way to do it.

The economists that push for these policies base their belief, to a significant extent, on the existence of high-unemployment rates that continue to prevail in many countries, and on the excess economic capacity that presumably also exists in these economies. For example, it has been reported that, in the USA, residential construction in 2012 was 49 percent below its historically determined level; spending on durable goods was 18 percent below the historical level; and spending on non-durable goods was also well below its historical trend. If the spending by these categories could be brought back to its historical trend, presumably by pushing aggregate demand through monetary or fiscal policy, the US economy could operate at a level of production that would be $764 billion higher than it was (see the article by Neil Irwin in the *Washington Post* of 30 October 2012, p. A16). The US economy has been estimated to be operating at this time (December 2012) at least 7 percent below its presumed potential. The fact that too many houses (and too many other goods) had been produced and could not be sold is ignored in these calculations.

In the view of the economists that hold these views, the excess capacity that now exists implies that the potential income is considerably higher than the actual income. They also believe that actual income could be raised simply by pushing the aggregate demand – regardless of the obstacles that are likely to exist to the use of the unemployed resources, and ignoring the mismatch between what the available resources are able to produce and the composition and not just the level of specific goods that the buyers would want to buy. These economists believe also that the existing conditions of high unemployment of labor and of excess capacity would be sufficient to prevent prices from rising at faster than desired, making the central banks' financing (and the larger fiscal deficit) kinds of *free lunches* for countries. This would simultaneously contribute to the salvation of the euro in Europe and to better economic conditions in the USA and UK.

Some past experiences, including that of Argentina in the 1980s, should be a warning for those who advocate these policies. In that decade Argentina underwent one of the *certified Great Depressions* of the twentieth century, when its real GDP fell by about 15 percent, creating a lot of unemployment and presumably a lot of excess capacity.

In that period the country also suffered a period of hyperinflation (see Tanzi, 2007a). Additionally, highly depressed economies in Europe in the 1970s, or transition economies in the 1990s, did not prevent prices in those countries from rising fast. In the case of the UK in the 1970s, prices rose at the fastest pace in that country's history.

The pressures on central banks to finance fiscal deficits, either directly or indirectly, have been only partly resisted by the European Central Bank and by the other central banks (including the Federal Reserve Bank and the Bank of England). As mentioned earlier, in the period of the Great Recession these central banks have acquired large amounts of government bonds, even bonds of countries that would have a hard time to repay them, such as Greece. They have also made large financial resources available, at very low rates, to private banks, by buying some of these banks' "assets" or allowing private banks to use assets of questionable value to get loans from the central banks. In the case of the US, this policy was at one time derided, or described, by Joe Stiglitz, as consisting of "cash for trash."

The policy has allowed the private banks to increase their holdings of government bonds, contributing to maintaining the interest rates on the governments bonds lower than they would have been otherwise, and increasing the earnings of the private banks. The policy has also increased the risks for the private banks, in the case of sovereign defaults by the relevant countries. These cross-countries financial links are now the focus of some of the difficulties that are attributed to the euro. Many German or French or Dutch private banks have been holding a lot of the public and private debt of the countries in difficulty, in particular Greece, Spain, and Portugal as well as some others. In the process some of the private banks that had been described as being "too big to fail" became even bigger, as a consequence of the public assistance, raising fears that a future financial crisis could have even more disastrous consequences than the recent one. In the USA, the implicit subsidies that these banks receive have been estimated by a Bloomberg analysis to be about $ 83 billion.

When the public bonds bought by banks are from countries other than those where the banks have their residence (French banks buying Greek government bonds, say, or French banks lending to Greek banks) the potential, cross-country spillover effects of policies are increased, because the size of *private* debt also becomes a concern for national policy, in addition to the size of *public* debt. This is a lesson that was learned in recent years when the level of private debt came also to be seen as a potential problem. The growth in cross-countries financial flows, excessive risks taken by large banks, and the inevitable incestuous connections that often exist between banks and governments could not fail to lead to problems, as happened in Ireland, Greece, Spain, Portugal, Cyprus and other countries. Some of the systemic risks were increased by the financial liberalization that was not accompanied by effective monitoring of banks and by efficient regulations.

This is especially the case now because of the complexity of many financial transactions and because of the growing role played by "shadow banking" in many of the transactions. Some countries (and their private banks) got into trouble because of their large exposure to developments in other countries. In several cases the sizes of these exposures were not known in advance. To some extent the current problems of the euro are the consequences of these spillover effects that were in turn and in part the consequence of the belief that the "no bailout clause" in the EMU rules would not be respected, so that the private banks could lend safely across the national borders to governments of EMU countries. This explains why Greece was able to borrow so much and at very attractive rates for several years before the crisis, in spite of the fact that there was growing evidence that its public finances were becoming progressively shakier. See, for example, Tanzi, 2007b, which, before the crisis, had questioned the veracity of the Greek public accounts data. Complexity plus lack of some relevant information and monitoring, together with false beliefs, were the major ingredients that led to the crisis. The BIS rules on capital requirements for banks also contributed to the problems by not requiring any holding of equity capital against the banks' holdings of government securities.

Some of the recent actions of the central banks have slowly transformed them into *quasi-fiscal and off-budget institutions*. The reason is that their function is no longer limited to the legitimate one of regulating money supply and price levels but has extended significantly into that of allocating cheap credit to particular sectors or activities, including government. This is a function that in a market economy should be left to the market and, to some extent, when intervention is needed to deal with market failures, to the public budget. It has become increasingly difficult, in recent years, to separate monetary from fiscal policy and thus to assess with some precision the objective fiscal stance of a country.

In the United States, in the past couple of years, the Fed bought $300 billion of Treasury bonds in QEI; $600-plus billion of Treasury bonds in QEII; and, in an operation called "twist," it has planned to buy $400 billion of long-term Treasury bonds, by selling shorter-term bonds, in the hope of pushing down the interest rates on long-term bonds, and thus stimulating demand for houses and to a lesser extent for cars. It has committed itself, for the time being, to continue buying huge assets ($85 billion) on a monthly basis. Jeffrey Lacker, the president of the Richmond Federal Reserve Bank, stated recently (September 2012) that: "Channeling the flow of credit to particular economic sectors [as the Fed has been doing] is an inappropriate role for the Federal Reserve." That channeling should be left to the private market and the Fed should not be in the business of financing public deficits.

The actions of the Fed have been creating some new bubbles in the bond market, which expose whoever buys these bonds (such as pension funds or personal savers), and especially those who buy the long-term bonds, at their current high prices to potentially large future losses, if – or, perhaps better, when – interest rates return, as they must, to the normal levels of the past.

Long-term real and nominal interest rates reached levels that in the United States and probably in some other countries had not been seen in 200 years. These levels could remain so low in the future only if the economy stopped growing. That would mean that the estimations of potential income for the United States and for some other countries, which are based on the performance of their economies in the past, before the Great Recession, and which, in the United States put potential income at levels around 7 percent above actual income, would have become meaningless. Using different growth rates would sharply increase the fiscal gaps mentioned earlier.

Similar objections to this fiscal role on the part of the European Central Bank have been raised by the German Central Bank, and by some other sources. However, the pressures on central bankers to show that they are doing something about the high unemployment and the depressed economic conditions, and, in Europe especially, the perceived need to "save the euro," have been too strong for central bankers to resist. Being human, central bankers respond to social and political pressures, just like all other humans. To many policymakers and observers, this intervention seems to be justified, especially in the short run, on the basis that it is necessary to facilitate, or make possible, the medium-run introduction of needed reforms. The short run is often favored over the long run by policymakers, and especially by those who tend to cite Keynes, that "in the long run we are all dead"! That is a powerful argument that makes the short run the preferred horizon for policies, and the short-run horizon is often determined by the period until the next elections.

There have been also pressures, on the few and declining number of European EMU countries that continue to have AAA ratings from the rating agencies, and especially on the largest of these countries, Germany, to create "firewalls" around the EMU countries that are facing major fiscal difficulties and high spreads. These firewalls would require the countries in good fiscal condition to take responsibility, through various schemes, for some of the risks that creditors run when they lend money to the countries in difficulty. Some believe that the very existence of these firewalls would be sufficient to lower the spreads so that the firewalls would not need to be used. There have been proposals, by some economists and political leaders, to issue "Eurobonds" on behalf of countries, bonds that would have shared European responsibility for their repayment. By sharing the responsibility, these bonds would carry lower interest rates and, thus, lower spreads for some countries. However, the *ex ante* sharing of the costs of future debt would also be a powerful incentive for less responsible governments to increase their borrowing.

# 4
# The Pressures on Germany to Help Save the Euro

There have been suggestions that Germany should pursue more expansionary fiscal and more relaxed labor policies than other EMU countries. Various economists, including Martin Wolf, a commentator with the *Financial Times*, Jean Pisani-Ferry, an economist at Bruegel (a think tank in Brussels), and some others, have been proponents of Germany's expansionary policies (see also the recent book in Italian by Mario Seminerio, 2012). In their views, by reducing the competitive advantage that Germany had acquired in recent years over some of the other EMU countries (because of the prudent policies that it had followed), expansionary policies followed by Germany, would improve the economic conditions for the whole European Monetary Union. The belief in the power of expansionary policies, even of indirect ones is, in part, behind these proposals.

The disequilibria that have come to exist in recent years, among the current account balances of EMU countries, and especially that between Germany and some of the EMU countries in difficulties, have been blamed for some of these countries' difficulties. It is in some sense implied that, if all countries had behaved as Greece, the trade imbalances and the accompanying capital movements across the EMU countries would not have developed, and neither would have the problems with the euro. Germany is guilty of having pursued too cautious, even if reasonable, policies. In this analysis, virtue seems to have been transformed into vice, or perhaps what is virtue for some is vice for others. For example, from the time of the EU Summit in Madrid in 1995, when the final decisions on the new monetary union were made, until 2008, when the financial crisis reached Europe, while prices grew by 67 percent in Greece, and

56 percent in Spain, they increased by only 9 percent in Germany and 26 percent for the whole euro area (data from Eurostat, reported in EEAG, 2012, p. 62).

This view, which assigns some blame to countries for having balance of payments surpluses, goes back a long time, to at least the Bretton Woods negotiations in 1944, where Lord Keynes argued that countries that experienced current account surpluses had some responsibilities in reducing the surpluses. This was consistent with the Keynesian view that the major problem for economic growth is essentially lack of demand and not, as would have been maintained by, for example, Schumpeter, that policies that distort the allocation of resources are more responsible for reducing the growth potential of countries. It has been part of the ideology of the past 70 years, which has given prominence to the demand side, while minimizing or ignoring the role played by the supply, which had been predominant before the Keynesian revolution.

The Keynesian view, which was slowly becoming an ideology, was that with enough demand, countries could grow, almost regardless of how distorted their policies became. We had to wait until the supply-side revolution of the 1980s before the supply side of the economy again received full attention and, for some conservative economists, to introduce a new and contrasting ideology, based on the view that higher taxes always have damaging effects on economic growth, and that often all that countries need to do to grow is to lower tax rates.

The Keynesian-based view of the role of balance of payments surpluses has also influenced, over the years, the debate between the USA (a deficit country) and China (a surplus country), on which country had the responsibility for eliminating the imbalance. In the 1980s and 1990s it also influenced the debate between the United States and Europe.

In this connection it may be worthwhile to remind the reader that it was not long ago, just about a decade ago, that Germany had been considered a country with economic difficulties, and almost the "sick man of Europe." It is ignored that the competitive advantage that Germany now has is a relatively recent development and the outcome of the good policies that it followed in *recent* years. Some might argue that perhaps the policies followed by Germany may have been too good, because they allowed limited growth of real wages and of prices, and kept good fiscal accounts.

As recently as 1989, Gerhard Fels, an important German economist, who was then the Director of the Institut der deutschen Wirtschaft, could write that

> Germany... is lagging far behind the United States and the United Kingdom in terms of economic revitalization. Rigidities, inflexibilities, and disincentives abound. [Therefore, Germany will require] major structural reforms... to generate the healthy investment climate, vital for [its] international competitiveness, in the 1990s.

Fels also warned that, without major reforms, Germany "might no longer be among the top industrial countries in another ten years." (See his contribution in Fels and von Furstenberg, 1989, p. 20.)

Some economists (see, for example, Seminerio, 2012, but also Martin Wolf at the *Financial Times*, Pisani-Ferry at Bruegel, and Hughes Hallett and Martinez Oliva at the Peterson Institute for International Economics) have seemed to suggest, in some of their writings, that the main problem in the European Monetary Union, and for the euro, is fundamentally the balance of payments problem, rather than the fiscal problem, a problem that some tend to minimize (see also EEAG, 2012, ch. 2). Thus, the solution to the problem would require changing the relative competitive positions of the EMU member countries, within the euro area. Make German goods more expensive for the Greeks, the Portuguese, or the Spaniards, and the goods of the latter countries cheaper for the Germans, and the euro problem would be solved! This puts the burden for the adjustment squarely on Germany, a view that has been gaining currency in the countries of Southern Europe, including in Italy, where Germany's popularity has clearly been damaged.

Interestingly, the relation between the price increases, in the EMU countries, between 1995 and 2008, and the current account balances, between 1995 and 2010, while it exists, is far from being a closed one. The correlation coefficient between the two variables is 0.52. Note that the data available, from the EEAG 2012 Report, for the current account balances extend the data for the price changes by two years. This extension is likely to have increased significantly the coefficient of correlation between these two variables. It is interesting that the two countries that had the largest price increases over the reported period (Slovenia and Slovakia) were far from those having had the largest current account imbalances. Furthermore, Luxembourg and the Netherlands, which had had price developments above the Euro area average, had the largest surpluses in their current account balances, surpluses even larger than Germany's. Therefore, the balance of payments story is far less convincing than it is made out to be, as an explanation of what went wrong in the EMU.

As mentioned, the competitive advantage of Germany was acquired in recent years, after many difficult years, when it had to absorb the much less developed and efficient East German part of Germany. The advantage gained was the direct outcome of prudent policies by the German government, policies that were aimed at making the German economy more efficient, as Professor Fels had wished more than a decade earlier. By contrast, the competitive disadvantage of various EMU countries was the result of bad policies, such as excessive wage and salary increases, large increases in public spending, little controlled foreign borrowing by the private sector, borrowing often used for consumption or for unproductive investment, and, in some of the countries, such as Spain, poor controls on the spending of sub-national governments. Bad regulations, which may have distorted the incentives and the efficiency of the economies, also played a significant role (see Giordano *et al.*, 2011). These policies were pursued after the bonanza (in terms of reduced inflation rates and interest rates) that several countries received after the coming into existence of the euro, and were followed for almost a decade.

In some cases, badly regulated or unregulated national banks, which had close relations with some political groups or parties within the countries, and which extended excessive credit to some politically favored sectors, especially the housing sector, as in Spain and in some other countries, played an important role. In Spain poorly controlled local governments and badly regulated banks contributed much to the future problems. If the euro area failed, it was for not having an EMU-wide regulatory system on the actions of the banks. There was no expansion and no bubble in the housing sector in Germany or in Italy, but in the latter there had been a significant increase in public spending over the years, some of it associated with higher salaries for public employees and financed by ad hoc measures.

The EMU is not a closed economy, with no, or limited, links with the outside world. Rather, its members, and especially the larger ones, trade significantly with the rest of the world, and the rest of the world is a much larger economic area, for any EMU country, than the rest of the EMU area. Therefore, making Germany less competitive *vis-à-vis* the poorly functioning EMU countries would also make it less competitive *vis-à-vis* the far more important rest of the world, and the rest of the world is not only a bigger area than the rest of the EMU but also a faster-growing one. It is doubtful if Germany would or should ever agree to run this risk, although it ought to be willing to reduce its high external surplus *vis-à-vis* the whole world if the current surpluses that it has been accumulating persist and do not generate significant benefits for it.

At the beginning of the financial crisis, there had been suggestions from various quarters of creating a European Monetary Fund, an institution that, like its more global counterpart in Washington, would provide financial assistance to the European economies that were in what were then believed to be temporary financial difficulties. These countries would avoid the need, or, for some, even, the embarrassment, of a European country going for assistance to the International Monetary Fund, an institution that for many years, until 2008, had mainly lent money to poorer, developing countries and for relatively short periods of time. The Fund programs of financial assistance were limited in time because it was assumed that a country that borrowed from the Fund would make the necessary economic reforms and adjustments in a relatively short period, thus allowing it to repay the IMF.

There has recently (October 2012) been created a €500 billion rescue fund (the European Stability Mechanism), financed by commitments from the member countries and from borrowing from the financial market, and backed by the guarantees of all the 17 EMU countries, in proportion to each country's economic power. (Thus the commitments by the four largest EMU countries would amount to 77.4 percent of the total, divided between Germany, 27.2 per cent; France, 20.2 percent; Italy, 17.9 percent; and Spain, 11.9 percent.) This has to some extent created an institution that bears some similarity to the IMF. The total financial capacity of the new institution, including some funds from previous programs is around €700 billion, which is not a small sum.

Furthermore, the lending power of the ESM, to particular EMU countries, could be beefed up by the bond-buying intervention in those countries by the ECB, provided that the countries were seen to be making needed policy changes – that is that they were adjusting. This development has created a European institution that, in some aspects and some functions, looks a lot like a *European* Monetary Fund. Such a Fund would provide *temporary* financial assistance to countries in difficulty, and would attach conditions to that lending, just as the IMF does. This conditionality would in principle reduce the possibility of moral hazard behavior by some countries' policymakers.

What remains to be seen is whether the European Stability Mechanism will have the needed technical capacity to do work similar to that done by the IMF, which has a large and experienced staff, to determine the conditions attached to the loans. The danger exists that the decisions (including the impositions of penalties where called for) may be influenced excessively by politics, because of the closeness of those who will make the decisions to those who will receive the loans. Horse-trading behavior may be a potential danger. This concern should receive the attention that it merits.

The creation of the ESM has not eliminated the role of the IMF in Europe. Today the International Monetary Fund finds itself in the situation, unthinkable just 5 years ago, in which a large share of its total financial resources is committed to European programs, and to programs within the EMU in which it is playing a major role in European decisions. The combination of the €500 (or €700) billion of the ESM, with the addition of possible ECB and IMF intervention, makes a lot of money potentially available to the European countries that might find themselves in *temporary* difficulties. This should allow them to make the needed reforms, and especially reforms related to the reduction of fiscal deficits, at an orderly but not too slow pace.

The assumption above is that the countries' difficulties are of a *temporary* nature, as some observers continue to believe, and can be dealt with through the use of temporary measures, such as the intervention of the ECB in the bond market. However, the basic thesis of this book is that the problems of several of the countries now in difficulty are not of a temporary or cyclical nature, but rather reflect excessive public spending that must be reduced to achieve more comfortable long-run positions and policies and institutions that excessively constrain some of the European economies. Therefore the problems of the euro are symptoms that signal deeper shortcomings. Without the needed reforms, especially those that reduce permanently public spending as a share of GDP, no amount of financial assistance would rescue the countries and the euro over the long run from their current predicaments.

The view expressed by many, that austerity could be abandoned in exchange for a strategy based on additional public spending, or immediate reductions in taxes, is a dangerous one. But, of course, over the medium run, significantly lower public spending, if achieved, should allow some countries to lower the high rates of some taxes that characterize them.

# 5
# The Fiscal Situation before the Crisis

In evaluating some of the various policies that have been proposed by experts to deal with the crisis, some important factors must be considered. Some of these are discussed briefly below.

The first factor is whether, before the 2008 crisis made its unwelcome apparition, the fiscal accounts of the countries that have been experiencing the greatest difficulties within the euro area were in what could be considered reasonably good shape. If this had been the case, it would have allowed the EMU countries to use the available "fiscal space" to help counteract the economic and social effects of the crisis on their economies. This aspect is important because many observers seem to believe that the fiscal difficulties now faced by various European countries (and by the euro) are the direct and immediate result of the financial crisis of 2008 – a crisis that initially came from the USA and that had its origin largely in the US housing market, as several good books on the crisis have highlighted. The authors of these books believe that the crisis was a kind of "random shock" for the European countries, which led to the current fiscal difficulties. If the sub-prime crisis had never happened in the USA, there would have been no problems for the European economies. They would have been able to go on merrily with their fiscal policies and with their high levels of public spending and taxes.

Another factor is whether the crisis that in 2008 and later years hit the countries' economies was in most countries of the traditional, garden-type, business-cycle variety, implicitly assumed by Keynesian economics; or whether it had different and specific features (for example difficulties in the banking system) that made it more difficult to deal with it with the help of a fiscal expansion – at least in some countries, including the United States. Both of the above factors may be important in determining whether there was scope for the use of an active and significant counter-cyclical fiscal policy (with the use of fiscal stimulus packages) after the crisis started, as some experts maintained.

Given (a) an initially prudent and sustainable fiscal situation, in a country that entered into an economic crisis, a situation that would be characterized by a low fiscal deficit, a low public debt, and a modest and easily sustainable tax burden; and (b) a recession of the traditional type, one characterized by the "weakening of animal spirits," that had led consumers and investors to become more pessimistic and, consequently, to spend and invest less – given these, then a Keynesian fiscal stimulus package, financed by easy credit and aimed at stimulating the economy, could, and, many would argue, should, be relied upon to help alleviate the effects on the economy of the reduction in aggregate spending. The stimulus package would inject additional demand into the economy and would assist the work of the automatic, built-in, fiscal stabilizers, which, for their impact on the economy, being automatic, do not require an *active* governmental intervention. Given the above assumptions, there would be a reasonable expectation that the (active) fiscal stimulus would help in reducing the negative impact of the recession on the countries' economies.

If used, an active fiscal stimulus package should be pursued with *temporary*, and easily *reversible*, increases in public spending and/or with *reversible*, or *temporary*, decreases in taxes in order to avoid future problems. This would prevent the fiscal stimulus from becoming a permanent increase in public spending. Investment on *needed* and ready-to-go infrastructure projects, projects that are ready, because they would have been built in any case in future years, that have passed a competent and careful evaluation of costs and benefits, and that could easily be brought forward in time, would be an example of reversible public spending that could be considered. Other examples could be temporary reductions (a) in the basic rate of the value added tax, to encourage private consumption, for countries that have such a tax; (b) in the excise taxes levied on expensive durable goods, such as cars and appliances, to encourage the anticipation of the purchase of such goods; or (c) in the first, basic, rate of the income tax, that is the rate that is most important to the majority of income tax payers and that is most likely to have the greatest impact on consumption.

The built-in, fiscal, stabilizers that are automatically activated by the weakening of the economy, such as higher unemployment compensation, lower tax payments because of reduction in incomes, and other similar programs, would widen the effects of the *discretionary* fiscal action. The effects of the fiscal *multipliers* would increase the total impact of the fiscal actions on the economy, especially for economies that are not excessively open, and when most individuals do not base their spending decisions on their *permanent* incomes, being liquidity-constrained. This is the situation generally and implicitly assumed by traditional, Keynesian stabilization policy. It is the textbook version of Keynesian, counter-cyclical, fiscal policy. Unfortunately, this version does not reflect the situation that existed in 2008 and later years in several of the European countries now in difficulties, or, for that matter, in the United States, the United Kingdom, and Japan.

Well before the 2008 crisis hit, the fiscal situation of many EMU and other countries was already highly precarious, especially when the anticipated impact of demographic trends on public spending, and the growing pressures in many countries to reduce their tax levels, were taken into account. Many countries had already high, and increasingly difficult-to-increase-further, average tax ratios (which, many economists and private operators were arguing, were damaging the growth rates of the economies), high and growing public debts, and significant fiscal deficits, within a context of positive economic growth (see Tanzi, 2011a). These fiscal developments had happened in spite of the fact that the ongoing bubbles, especially those in housing and in the financial market, had been artificially inflating the growth rates and the tax revenues of several of the countries, thus providing a misleading impression of what would be the bubble-free reality (see Tanzi, 2012b). Furthermore, as we shall be arguing below, various accounting devices that the countries' governments had been using had contributed to the illusion, on the part of unwary observers, that the public accounts of several countries were in better shape than they were in reality.

The ratios of public debts to GDPs – even as officially measured, which, as we shall argue later probably underestimated the real situations of the fiscal accounts in many countries – had been growing significantly years before the crisis, especially, but not only, in the EMU countries. A "comment" that the author of this book had published, on 12 August 2003, in the Comments and Analysis section of the *Financial Times*, on the basis of ongoing trends (which at that time were already clearly visible to well-trained fiscal observers in several industrial countries and not just in EMU countries), had warned about the growing possibility of *future fiscal crises*. The bubbles that had started developing around the year 2003, that were financed by extremely cheap interest rates and encouraged by lax regulatory controls on banks and on some activities, together with lack of good statistical information on some variables, had obscured to some extent the fiscal developments, but also more generally the financial ones. As a recent article in the *Financial Times* put it, "banking products have grown so complex and the strategies employed by traders so mystifying, that only someone who has taken part in the financial alchemy can oversee it" (see Jonathan Ford, *FT*, 2 July 2012, p. 9; also Tanzi, 2007c, for an earlier and similar warning). Unfortunately the same could be said about *fiscal* products. Thus complexity in the financial market had been added to the complexity in the fiscal situation, as described below, and to the lack of good regulations at a global or regional level that had stimulated much regulatory arbitrage by banks and increased potential dangers for economies.

As mentioned earlier, the bubbles and the effects of the low interest rates had inflated the tax revenue and probably had also created some artificial economic growth in several countries, including the United States and the United Kingdom, besides having lowered the costs of servicing the public debts (and the financing of private borrowing; see Tanzi, 2012b). The bubble-free growth rates, before 2008, would have been lower, and the fiscal deficits would have been higher, *ceteris paribus*, in the absence of the bubbles. These developments would also distort the measures of the excess capacity of the countries' economies during the Great Recession and the measure of potential income for the years after the crisis, which is important in estimating the present value of future fiscal developments assuming no changes in policies. The lower are the future growth rates, the larger become the present values of the fiscal gaps.

When some of the European countries started discussing the establishment and the characteristics of a European Monetary Union (EMU), in the first half of the decade of the 1990s, following the

Delors Report of 1989, there had been large differences in some relevant variables among those countries. The inflation rates, the interest rates, the levels and the structures of public spending and of public revenue, and the levels of fiscal deficits and public debts, had been significantly different among the potential member countries. (For the differences in interest rates see figure 2.3 on p. 61 of *EEAG Report 2012*.) Furthermore, the reputations of the countries' policymakers were also widely different, with the German central bank having established by far the best reputation because of its good management of monetary policy over previous years, which had produced the lowest inflation in that country. (The memory of past episodes of inflation had made the Germans and their central bank particularly allergic to policies that could lead to inflation.) The German representatives in the negotiations, therefore, pressed for the use of specific rules that would constrain the policymakers of other countries as well as those of Germany. The rules proposed would become the Maastricht rules, or the rules in the Stability and Growth Pact.

Some of the differences between countries in the relevant variables were seen to be potentially damaging to the functioning of a monetary union. It was thus understood that the monetary *club* to which the EMU countries would belong, the European Monetary Union, could not allow the continuation of these differences (see Tanzi, 2004). The differences were particularly large in the reported sizes of the fiscal deficits and in the shares of the public debts into GDPs. There were also differences among countries, and even within countries, between the measurements made by central banks and those made by treasuries or by statistical offices, on the fiscal variables. In 1992, Mervyn King, who later would become the governor of the Bank of England, had called attention to the "enormous conceptual and measurement problems... in measuring, comparing, and even defining budget deficits across countries..." (King, 1992, p. 261). King's concern, which was shared by other experts, could lead to major problems for a monetary union if it were not addressed.

In 1995, the European Union, through the European System of National and Regional Accounts (ESA 95), provided some official guidelines to be followed, starting in mid 1999, by all the 27 EU member countries. The new guidelines would allow a better comparison of the fiscal variables of the different European countries. From 2000 on, the ESA 95 figures became the reference for budgetary surveillance in

Europe and especially in the part of Europe that consisted of the EMU countries. The use of these guidelines would, in principle, remove or reduce the possibility that different criteria, used by different member countries, could distort and invalidate the cross-countries comparisons of the fiscal variables that were estimated by the countries' experts and were reported to the European Commission for its evaluation of the countries' policies.

Unfortunately, the new criteria still left various conceptual gray areas on how to classify some fiscal actions, giving scope to the possibility of opportunistic reporting, by some countries, of variables that had become politically important and for which incentives to make them look better than they were had become stronger. "Goodhart's law," so called, which broadly states that "when the value of a variable creates incentives for its manipulation, that value will be manipulated," became clearly relevant for some fiscal statistics (see Goodhart, 1975).

# 6
# The EMU Rules and Goodhart's Law

Neither the measurement of fiscal deficits nor that of public debts is like the measurement of a person's weight or height, for which there are clear, objective standards for measurements. It is often not easy to connect fiscal deficits with changes in public debt. The IMF has recently dealt *again*, officially, with the difficult question of "fiscal transparency," because in its own words "the degree of fiscal transparency has been shown to be an important predictor of a country's fiscal credibility and performance" (see IMF, 2012b, p. 5).

The recent IMF paper has pointed out that "fiscal transparency is a critical element of effective fiscal policymaking and the management of fiscal risks" (*ibid.*, p. 3). This "critical element" had been a perennial problem for IMF financial programs with countries during the 27 years that the author of this book spent at the IMF. Countries would often present data that were not right in their attempt to convince the staff of the IMF that they were adjusting their fiscal accounts, as had been required by the so-called "letters of intent," the formal document that set the conditions for getting financial assistance from the IMF, while Fund staff would try to discover the tricks that had been used. It was a cat-and-mouse game that, at times, led to the suspension of financial programs with some countries because of these problems. The fact that in 2012 the IMF Board of Executive Directors of the IMF still felt the need to return to this problem means that the doubts raised by Mervyn King in 1992 have not disappeared.

The European Commission assumed that, in the preparation of the fiscal data the officials of the European countries would follow, honestly and competently, the guidelines that had been provided in 1995 by Eurostat. They also assumed, that the officials would report correctly to the European Commission the countries' estimates of the fiscal deficits, the public debts and other important statistics. The European Commission did not itself have the mandate to do that work; nor, for that matter, did it have the manpower necessary and sufficient to monitor closely the estimations made by the national authorities, in the large number of countries that were members of and that reported to the EU. Its presence in the countries was limited to occasional contacts in Brussels or not frequent visits to the countries. Inevitably, it had to rely on the reporting by the countries' authorities and had to assume that that reporting was accurate and honest.

This situation, of course, created the possibility (anticipated by Charles Goodhart for monetary statistics) that some governments might not be as honest in their reporting, or as competent in their estimates, as it would be desirable. They might hide or delay the payment on, some public spending, or the reporting of it, or anticipate the collection or inflate the reporting of some public revenue; or they might use accounting devices that would make it possible to report results that looked better than they were objectively. For example the reimbursement of the VAT to exporters, or the payment of money due to private enterprises that had done works for the public sector, could be delayed and thus affect some of the measures of the fiscal deficits or public debts that were reported. Or financial engineering tricks could be used. A detailed account of these difficulties, at the time when EMU was being set up, was presented in various papers published in an Italian book (see Ragazzi, 1997). Other papers mentioned in the reference section in this book indicate that over the years this had become a significant problem for the EMU countries. There is no doubt, and much indirect evidence, that various accounting devices were used, either immediately before the creation of the EMU in order to qualify to become a member, or in the later years to avoid penalties. Both of the above situations had become powerful incentives for the use of Goodhart's law.

In the years immediately before the coming into existence of the EMU, the authorities of some countries relied on various tricks, and hid various skeletons, in order to qualify for membership. These skeletons would in later years come out of the proverbial closets. In the years after the creation of EMU the tricks were used to escape the penalties, until the Maastricht rules were changed in the mid 2000s. At times, sales of public assets to off-budget but government-controlled institutions were counted as immediate, ordinary revenue. Future streams of revenue were subject to "cartolization," that is they were sold against immediate payments that would count as revenue. The definition, and the treatment of, "public enterprises," enterprises that were fully or partly controlled by the governments, was also a problem in determining whether they were part of general government so that their costs and revenues could be taken into account in the fiscal estimates. The government could influence the timing of the distribution of dividends by profitable, publicly controlled enterprises. In some sectors, such as the public health sector, the spending could only be estimated for the current year, because it would take much longer before the actual spending was known, and the actual spending was often higher than the estimated figures. (See Reviglio, 2001, for some information on the Italian experience.)

Recently, an interesting, recent paper by a staff member of the IMF has shown that this has been a common problem among countries and not one limited to those in the EMU (see Irwin, 2012). However, among EMU countries the power of the incentives in Goodhart's law may have been stronger. That paper has provided a useful classification of the ways in which countries have used the accounting devices. The main categories are the following:

(a) *Hidden borrowing,* of which different kinds are possible. One example is when governments take over pension schemes of private companies or of public enterprises, at a time when the cash flow of the pension schemes is favorable to the government. The pension contributions, or even the accumulated assets of the private pensions, then count as revenue for the budget while the future pension payments do not. Countries such as Austria, Belgium, Denmark, France, Sweden, and Portugal have been reported to have used this device in Europe at some point in time. Other countries, as for example Argentina in the 1990s, have done so in other regions. Recently Poland was also reported to be considering such a takeover. Another example is the sale and leaseback of government-owned property including buildings used as ministries. Still another is the use of swaps, to hedge against financial risks. Greece, Belgium, Germany, and Italy are reported to have used such strategies. Often these countries have been assisted in these complex operations by well-known and well-compensated global investment banks.

(b) *Disinvestment,* which also increases current revenue but (often but not always) also increases future costs to the government. According to Irwin: "Germany's effort to satisfy the criteria for adoption of the euro in late 1990s was aided by...the sale of railway land..." (p. 8). Italy liquidated most of the assets of IRI (the Istituto per la Ricostruzione Industriale). Portugal and Belgium are reported to have securitized tax receivable. In some cases, "the transactions were effectively loans to the government" (*ibid.*). In many countries, including Japan, many assets were privatized not because it was necessarily a good policy but in order to get revenue. In Italy some public monopolies became private monopolies. In some countries providing the monopoly status to the new private owners allows the government to get higher revenue from the sales.

(c) *Deferred spending.* Policies that delayed the cash payments when they were due reduced the current fiscal deficits while probably increasing future ones. For example, in 2012 there was an intense discussion in Italy about tens of billions of euros owed to enterprises that had done projects for the public sector but had not been paid when the work was done. This delay had reduced the government cash deficit but had increased the enterprises' difficulties. Many examples are reported in the Irwin paper, including a table that for five Anglo-Saxon countries shows the large differences, especially in the UK and US, that in 2010 existed between officially measured public debt and total public sector liabilities.

(d) *Foregone investments.* This category is a more controversial one. It refers to public investments that need to be made but that the government does not make and shifts the responsibility to private operators through so-called "public–private partnerships (PPP)." Private enterprises put up the capital and operate the infrastructure facilities for a number of years, but the government, which has saved the initial cost of the projects, assumes "contingent liabilities" by often guaranteeing a given rate of return to the private investors. These future contingent liabilities, which do not appear in the budget, put the government at risk, as the title of an important World Bank book put it (see Polackova *et al.,*

2002). There is no question that by entering into these agreements the government reduces its own immediate spending on the investments, while it assumes the risk of high future costs. The literature dealing with these issues indicates that often the future costs to governments tend to be higher than anticipated in the original contracts. It also indicates that these contracts often, or occasionally, lead to acts of corruption because low bids are submitted with some implicit or hidden agreement that in the future the contract will be adjusted at times after some modification in the project.

(e) *Disappearing government.* In this category of accounting devices to show better current fiscal accounts, "[public] spending [is] undertaken by a public entity that is not counted as part of the government for reporting purposes" (Irwin, p. 11). For example, Greece had pushed the bus, railway, and some other companies that made large losses out of the government, to show lower public spending. Eurostat reclassified them as public enterprises, thus adding 7.8 percent of GDP to the Greek public debt. Similar accounting devices have been used by other countries, especially in connection with losses connected with banking crises.

Well-paid experts from foreign financial enterprises (in the case of Greece, from Goldman Sachs) or other foreign advisers were hired, over the years, by some governments to assist them with developing accounting and financial engineering tricks that made it possible for some countries to report fiscal results that looked better than they should have looked or that they were. As mentioned earlier, complexity and lack of transparency was not a problem just for the private financial market; it had progressively become a major problem for governments, and it affected the measurement of statistics, when that measurement had some important consequences. In some ways the growing importance of the statistics, especially of the fiscal deficit and the public debt, led to the manipulation of the estimates. Additionally, actual spending was increasingly replaced by the governments' assumption of contingent liabilities, liabilities that might be costly in the future, but which were generally not reported in the countries' budgets.

In some cases, as in Greece, and to a lesser extent in other countries, including Italy, there were occasional revisions made by the European

Commission in the public accounts that had been reported by the countries in earlier years. These revisions could at times amount to several percentage points of GDP. Some of these revisions were due to the later, and more accurate, availability of some expenses, such as those connected with the public health sector that, as mentioned earlier, are only known precisely some time after they are made. However, in some cases there may have been less honest reasons for the earlier underreporting. The annual impact of "one-off measures," measures that affect only the accounts of one year, such as the sale of a public asset, of "creative accounting," and of "reclassification" for the important period between 1993 and 2003 is shown in a figure on p. 13 of the Irwin paper. The correlation between these annual estimates and the "spreads" in January 2011 for the countries in financial difficulties is remarkable.

In Greece the share of total government revenue into GDP was reported to have risen by more than 6 percentage points between 1995 and 2000, while the share of total expenditure had hardly changed and was reported to have even fallen until 2005–06. It exploded in the next couple years, even before the financial crisis had its effect. The expenses connected with the hosting of the 2004 Olympics were probably significantly underreported at the time they were made. They amounted to as much as 5 percent of GDP.

In Italy, the total expenditure of the general government was reported to have fallen, by 6.4 percentage points of GDP, between 1995 and 2000. This fall led to a reduction in the Italian fiscal deficit of 6.6 percent of GDP, allowing Italy to become one of the original members of the European Monetary Union. In December 2004 there was a controversy between the Italian government and representatives of the European Commission. It had to do with large differences in the measurement of the fiscal deficit, between the Italian central bank and the Italian treasury. The controversy related to different interpretations of particular fiscal actions by the two institutions. It attracted the attention of the Commission but it is not clear how it was resolved.

In these debates between the European Commission and the national governments the interpretations by national governments have normally aimed at reducing the size of the measured fiscal deficit or of the public debt, while those of the Commission have tended to increase it. The revisions made to the accounts have not been random but almost always have been in one direction: toward a worsening of the earlier-reported fiscal accounts.

Thus, a *club* (the European Monetary Union) had been created that, regardless of the quality of its formal rules, was faced from the very beginning by the danger that the individual member countries would not always honestly follow the agreed rules, or honestly report the true fiscal outcomes. This created the conditions for future problems, because it reduced the true fiscal space that the countries had when the American financial crisis landed in Europe in 2008. It also seemed to confuse many macroeconomists who had not spent much time in the dirty room where fiscal statistics were created. Some have continued to repeat that the fiscal accounts before the crisis of various EMU countries (and some others) were not a concern.

In 1995, at the time when the creation of a European Monetary Union was being contemplated, the reported net lending of the general government (the officially accepted measure of the fiscal deficit) among the future EMU countries ranged from a reported *surplus* of 2.4 percent of GDP in Luxembourg to a reported *deficit* of 9.1 of GDP in Greece and 7.4 percent in Italy. The measures of the ratio of gross public debts to GDP ranged from a low of 7.4 percent in Luxembourg to a high of 130.2 percent in Belgium. In Italy it was 120.9 percent, and in Greece it was 97.9 percent. Total tax revenue, as a percentage of GDP, was also widely divergent: it ranged from 29.4 for Greece to 43.7 for Belgium, and 42.7 for France. It should be noted that in later years Belgium was successful in reducing significantly its public debt, from 130.2 percent of GDP in 1995 to 84.0 percent in 2007, generally through good policies, without paying a high price in terms of its economic growth. Its debt to GDP ratio went up again after the crisis.

A monetary union could not tolerate the large differences in fiscal deficits and public debts reported above. Therefore, there was the need for some coordination of policies among the countries, and for some leveling of the existing differences, before the monetary union could become operative. Coordination could, in principle, be achieved through market-based discipline, or else would need specific rules.

At that time, some economists believed that the assignment of different ratings to countries, by official rating agencies, would be enough to force the needed policy coordination among the countries.

Poorer ratings would increase the cost of borrowing for governments that had greater fiscal imbalances, increasing for them the cost of borrowing and, presumably, reducing their incentives to borrow. If this occurred, then rating agencies, or the spontaneous pressures of the market forces, would generate the needed fiscal corrections, without the need for explicit rules. Some believed that this kind of coordination happened in the US, especially in the municipal bond market, where the ratings, by the rating agencies, brought about significant differences in the interest rates that were paid by municipalities (see on this the paper by Goldstein and Woglom, 1992). However, there was skepticism on whether this market-based discipline would actually achieve what was expected of it (see the comments, on Goldstein and Woglom's paper, by King and by Tanzi, in the book edited by Canzoneri *et al.*, 1992).

The officials who made the decisions on the rules that the EMU countries would have to follow concluded that, realistically, market forces would not be able to do the required job, in particular because the time horizons of governments in democracies are always limited. At times, the next elections can be won by the government in power by promising more spending, to benefit particular clienteles, and by pursuing short-run expansionary policies, while leaving for a later time, or for a later government, the problem of correcting the fiscal accounts. In this political cycle, the horizons of governments generally do not extend much beyond the time of the next elections.

The alternative that was chosen by the governments' representatives, under pressures from the Germans, was to promote the needed coordination among countries though *fiscal rules* (the so-called Maastricht, or Stability and Growth Pact, rules) which were endorsed by the governments of the EMU countries. In what may have been an initial mistake, the observance of these rules did not require the endorsement of the countries' parliaments. The European Commission would monitor the observance of the rules, and the rules would apply to the reported official measure of the fiscal deficits and of the shares of the public debts of the general governments into the countries' GDPs. Financial penalties were contemplated for countries that violated the rules to create some incentives for observing them. However, the penalties were not automatic; their application was supposed to be endorsed by the representatives of the member countries that would act as a pressure group. It was also assumed that the governments would have collective incentives to follow the rules.

Another possible mistake, made at the beginning, was that the fiscal rules did not limit the countries' shares of public spending and of tax revenue into their GDPs. These shares were seen to be the political prerogative of the countries' governments, as long as the governments did not violate the Maastricht rules on the size of the deficit and the public debt. Therefore, different countries could choose or maintain the economic role of the state (and, thus, the shares into GDP of spending and taxes) that they favored. This meant that, in 2007, for example, France had a level of public spending that was 9 percent of GDP higher than that of Germany, and a tax burden that was 4.4 higher. These differences could not fail to have an impact on the relative performances of these countries over the years, thus creating problems of coordination.

The agreed fiscal rules would apply to the shares of fiscal imbalances and public debts into the countries' GDPs. It should be noted that, by not requiring the parliaments to endorse the rules, and by not setting limits to total public spending, as this latter rule existed in a few European countries, including the Netherlands, potential future problems were being created. The author of this book was surprised at how little attention the Italian government, which came into power in June 2001, paid to these rules, at the time when he was part of that government (June 2001–July 2003).

A convenient rule, but one not easy to follow, at least on a yearly basis, could have been the adoption of "Cicero's rule," as advocated 2000 years ago by the famous Roman statesman and politician. It was a rule that over the centuries had provided some guidance, at least in principle, to the behavior of governments. It had been endorsed, in some limited form, by the majority of "states" within that other monetary union that is the United States of America, after many of them had got into difficulties in the nineteenth century, so creating the need for fiscal discipline at the state level. The Cicero rule is essentially a balanced-budget rule, but in its original Cicero version it was not necessarily related to the budget outcome in that arbitrary period of time that, in today's world, has become one year, the period normally used today in public and private budgets.

The Cicero rule is a rule that over the 20 centuries since it was formulated had generally been endorsed, if not always followed, by responsible governments. In the year 43BC, Cicero had written:

> The national budget must be balanced. The public debt must be reduced. The arrogance of the authorities must be moderated and controlled. Payments to foreign governments must be reduced if the nation does not want to go bankrupt. People must again learn to work, instead of living on public assistance.

This statement could be accepted, without modifications, by today's governments. The EMU would have been wise to adopt it, in spite of the Goodhart problem which has been emphasized by economists such as von Hagen (1991) and Poterba (1995). At the urging of Germany, the European Monetary Union has recently been moving in the direction of the Cicero rule. It remains to be seen how much it will move, and, if adopted, how well the rule will work.

The Cicero rule had been backed, over the centuries, by prominent personalities, including David Hume, George Washington, and in more recent years by, among others, Jacques de Larosière when he was the managing director of the IMF (1982) and at a time when there was not much concern about public debt. As Hume had put it, three centuries ago:

> The practice... of contracting debt will almost infallibly be abused in every government... Therefore... the consequences... must indeed, be one of... two events; either the nation must destroy public credit, or public credit will destroy the nation. (Hume, 1955)

George Washington believed that "There is no practice more dangerous [for a government] than that of borrowing money."

As mentioned, the Cicero rule was accepted and included in the constitutions of most of the states of the United States in the nineteenth century to prevent the states from abusing their borrowing power, a problem that is common in federations. In spirit the Cicero rule requires the balancing of the budget, if not every year then at least over some longer period, or over the business cycle. It also requires implicitly that public debts be kept low or close to zero because sudden changes in interest rates can lead to sudden changes in fiscal deficits when the shares of debt into GDP are high. The guiding principles of the Cicero rule were: (a) borrowing should be temporary; (b) it should be caused by extraordinary events; and (c) it should be repaid as soon as possible so that public debts do not accumulate.

The balanced-budget rule obviously conflicted with the Keynesian orthodoxy that became widely accepted after World War Two and that, in spite of some academic criticism of it, especially in the 1970s, was still prevalent in the 1990s, notably in official circles. Keynesian economics had convinced many economists and political leaders that, by increasing demand and thus creating presumably favorable winds for the movements of economies, fiscal deficits helped promote faster economic growth, even in normal times. Therefore fiscal deficits were not just useful to fight occasional recessions, but they were useful in a world in which deficient demand is supposed to be the norm, thus creating fiscal space for governments to exploit. This view would provide the slippery slope that would lead many countries to the current fiscal difficulties, and not just the members of the European Monetary Union.

The balanced-budget rule had been sharply criticized, after the advent of Keynesian economics, in the late 1940s and 1950s, by several of the major economists of the time, including Paul Samuelson, James Tobin and other economists who would receive a Nobel prize in later years when the Prize was established. It was seen as a rule that removed the discretion over budgetary policy that presumably wise and unbiased policymakers, who have the welfare of the community in mind, should have. Many of the top economists of the 1940s and 1950s, who had lived through the Great Depression, considered the balanced-budget rule a dangerous relic of the past. For example, James Tobin, who would later win the Nobel prize in economics, wrote in the late 1950s that "Orthodox fiscal doctrines [that is, balanced budgets] have... brought the nation [the USA during the Eisenhower administration] to the brink of catastrophe" (see Tobin, 1966, p. 57).

Keynesian economics had made fiscal deficits appear modern and almost virtuous. They were seen as offering desirable free lunches to governments who had much appetite for more public spending at a time when the desired economic role of the state was changing rapidly and that were happy to have excuses for spending more. The politicians were provided free lunches similar to the ones now offered by some economists, through the financing of public spending by means of monetary expansion. This latter policy, which helps finance fiscal deficits through monetary expansion, can combine the free lunch of fiscal policy with the free lunch of monetary policy, to offer a real banquet.

On the other hand, balanced budgets and low public debts had come to be seen as ancient and dangerous relics especially if enforced on a yearly bases. Keynesianism had made the pursuit of balanced budgets look definitely primitive and wrong-headed, and those trying to promote them the followers of dead economists who, by being dead, must have been dead wrong. It was not surprising that these attitudes, which dominated the thinking of many of the government officials who negotiated the Maastricht Treaty, would influence the rules that the EMU chose (see Tanzi, 2007b).

Unfortunately, discretion for policymakers often does not work as well, as some of the earlier Keynesian economists had predicted. Decisions that influence fiscal policy outcomes may be influenced by (a) electoral cycles; (b) common pool problems; (c) the role of bureaucracies; (d) political biases toward current generations; (e) favorable biases toward large governments; (f) asymmetric behavior by policymakers over the cycle; (g) the inability of financial markets to send the right signals to the countries' policymakers; (h) principal agents problems and corruption – and so on. Whatever the reasons, it is clear that discretion often has not worked as well as it had been assumed by the earlier supporters of Keynesian fiscal policy. For this reason, in more recent years, rules that would hopefully be efficient and enforceable have become popular. In some ways and with due changes this could be considered a return to Cicero. Many countries have recently established "fiscal councils" to promote and enforce fiscal rules, realizing that fiscal discretion has not delivered the results that had been expected in the immediate post Keynesian period.

# 7
# On Public Debts, Fiscal Deficits, and the Maastricht Rules

An empirical study co-authored by the author of this book – written for a seminar on public debt and fiscal policy in EMU, held at the European Commission in Brussels on 17 September 1999 at a time when EMU had just become official – concluded that: "A growing public debt appears to lead to higher direct taxes, lower public investment and, ultimately, a lower growth rate. In addition, higher debt does seem to crowd out private capital formation and raise interest rates." It added, "[E]vidence for the EU suggests that it is possible [that] lower debt will have non-negligible [positive] effects on growth rates..." Therefore, "[T]he welfare impact over time of lowering public debt could be large" (see Tanzi and Chalk, 2000, p. 41). The conclusions of that study were ignored at the time they were presented and for several years afterwards, even by economists interested in the topic. Only many years later, when public debt started to attract attention, were those conclusions endorsed or challenged by various studies that had consistently failed to cite it.

Recent work by several scholars has largely shared the conclusions, reached a decade earlier, by the above-mentioned study. The view that high public debt may reduce economic growth has recently been backed by studies by Reinhart and Rogoff (2010 and 2011b), Kumar and Woo (2010), Baldacci and Kumar (2010), Ali Abbas *et al.* (2010), Mauro *et al.* (2013), Egert (2013) and others. There is, however, no agreement as to the level of public debt at which it begins to significantly reduce the countries' rates of growth. In 2013 a tempest in a teapot exploded over some rather trivial mistakes made by Reinhart and Rogoff in their much-cited 2010 paper that had largely confirmed the conclusions of the Tanzi and Chalk paper of a decade earlier.

Some challenged their conclusion that a 90 percent of GDP was a critical level for the debt. Of course such a level cannot be established for all countries and for all times because it depends on the use made of the money and the cost of borrowing. In this debate many critics, including Krugman, confused the short-run economic impact of fiscal expansions with the impact on long-run growth.

In the first decade of the new millennium, the public debts of many countries, especially in Europe but also including Japan, rose to reach very high and potentially dangerous levels. The current levels of debt in many countries are likely to have entered the danger zone. One wishes that the conclusions of the Tanzi and Chalk study had been wrong; or, if right, that they had attracted some attention *at the time they were presented,* in what had been an important meeting, and in what should have been a highly visible publication of the European Commission, namely *European Economy – Reports and Studies,* no. 2: *Public Debt and Fiscal Policy in EMU,* 2000.

The framers of the Stability and Growth Pact in 1997 tried to integrate the need for fiscal convergence within the EMU countries, a convergence that was felt to be necessary for the success of the monetary union, with the prevailing Keynesian orthodoxy. Therefore, the EMU countries were allowed to have fiscal deficits up to 3 percent of GDP, and public debts up to 60 percent of GDP.

For the rule concerning the fiscal deficits, the assumption had been, or a favorable *ex post* interpretation could be, that governments would aim to keep their fiscal deficits, in normal economic times, close to zero and that the governments of the countries would understand that the 3 percent limit was a *ceiling,* capable of providing ample fiscal space for the countries that in normal times had maintained their fiscal deficits close to zero. This would give them the possibility of using a Keynesian fiscal expansion, in case of recessions, by allowing the fiscal deficit to rise up to the 3 percent limit. A fiscal space of 3 percent of GDP should have been sufficient to allow the countries to engage in adequate countercyclical policy in the cyclical circumstances that were most common, but the *normal* deficit should have been close to zero.

However, the 3 percent limit soon became the normal *target* for the countries' fiscal deficits, rather than the *ceiling* to be reached, but not surpassed, during recessions. Thus, when in the early years of the twentieth century the rates of growth of some of the countries slowed down and, because of the impact of the slowdown on the fiscal account, the fiscal deficits rose above 3 percent of GDP – in Portugal (2001 and 2005), France (2002 and 2003), Germany (2002), Netherlands (2003), Italy (2004), and Greece (2005) – these countries became potentially liable to financial sanctions.

The penalties would be applied by the Council of Ministers of the countries, upon the recommendations of the European Commission. Punitive actions were started twice, against Portugal (in 2002) and Greece (in 2005), but they were never applied. It became evident that the Commission seemed more ready to go after small countries, but was much more reluctant to go after bigger violators, such as France and Germany, which were seen as "too big to penalize." The penalties for violating the budget rule were thus not applied, and there was the beginning of a push to revise the Stability and Growth Pact so as to make it more user-friendly. France and Germany led the push to change the rule, with some backing from Italy. They argued that the violation of the fiscal rule had been justified by the economic slowdown that had increased the deficits and had also created a need to increase aggregate demand. They asked for a more flexible use of the rules. Many Keynesians endorsed the call.

The Commission received many suggestions from economists on how to revise the Maastricht rules. These suggestions ranged from calls to use a so-called "golden rule," that would exclude from the public spending investment expenses (in some more sophisticated versions adjusted for the depreciation of the public infrastructures) to measure the fiscal deficit that would be considered relevant, to calls for the use of the "net worth of the public sector" as the relevant variable. The suggestions received by the Commission, some from well-known economists, varied from the very simple and practical to the very complex and highly impractical.

The original Maastricht rules were revised in 2005. The revisions were in the direction of making the rules even less stringent than they had been, and the countries even less fiscally constrained (see Tanzi, 2008a, for details). The main changes made to the rules can be best described by citing a 2006 paper, presented by Almunia, then commissioner responsible for economic developments at the European Commission, to a conference in Poland:

> The preventive dimension of the Pact has been strengthened by a stronger and more differentiated medium-term orientation of the rules. [In the future] the medium-tem budgetary objective of a

> country will be defined on the basis of its current debt ratio and *potential* growth... [C]ountries with a combination of low debt and high *potential* growth will be able to run a small [fiscal] deficit *over the medium run*, whereas a balanced budget or a surplus will be required for countries with... high debt and low potential growth. (Almunia, 2006; italics added)

The Commission and the Council, the text continues, would take into account factors such as "developments in *potential* growth and prevailing *cyclical* conditions..." (italics added).

The new rules introduced *potential growth* and the *structural deficit* as relevant variables, replacing the *actual* fiscal deficit and the *actual* GDPs, for the application of the Maastricht rule. As a consequence of these changes they also introduced a lot of discretion. These changes must have looked to many observers as being in the right direction, and were generally welcome. The problem was that the estimation of the *structural* deficit and of *potential* growth depends on arbitrary assumptions about the past and future developments of a country and about the size of the excess capacity of its economy during a slowdown or a downturn. These variables are not known, and cannot be known objectively. As a recent IMF study has admitted: "declines in 'potential' (or long-run) economic growth may not be fully apparent in real time to contemporary policymakers..." It would be a mistake, for example, to estimate today the future growth of the US on the basis of the pre-crisis economic growth, as some measures of current potential income continue to do. Therefore, the new rules essentially replaced *real* variables with *virtual* variables. In lacking objectivity the new rules lent themselves to easier manipulation.

This change in the rules must have contributed to the progressive weakening of the public finances that was already taking place in several of the EMU countries that, even before the crisis, accompanied the progressively easier monetary polices that had been common at that time. In some countries, before the financial crisis, the bubbles and the manipulation of the fiscal data hid the fiscal weakening that had been taking place, a weakening that has continued to elude the attention of some recent commentators that have continued to repeat that the fiscal accounts were not a problem.

As to the specific rule concerning the public debt, when the Maastricht Treaty had been agreed, the problem had been that several countries had had shares of officially measured public debts into GDP that were well over 60 percent. Some, such as Belgium, Greece, and Italy, had public debts much above 60 percent of GDP. They obviously could not bring their debts down to the required level overnight or in a short time period. These countries were asked to lower their public debt ratios towards the 60 percent target, in a reasonable time and in a progressive way.

This rule or requirement was soon forgotten and the public debts, which in the years of preparation toward Maastricht had in some countries started to be reduced – at least in their official measures, which were affected by large sales of public assets – soon resumed the upward trend that they had had in previous years, in spite of further accounting tricks that several countries continued to use. In Germany, France, Portugal, and some other countries the debt to GDP ratio increased as a percentage of GDP in the years of the new millennium, before the financial crisis arrived. By contrast, the debt/GDP ratio went sharply down in Belgium, a country that, perhaps because it hosted the European Commission, seemed to pay more serious attention to the Maastricht rules.

In the 20 years before 1997, the combined public debts of the original EMU countries had risen from 31.1 percent of GDP in 1977, to 75.4 percent of GDP in 1997, surely a very large increase. This had also been the period when the shares of tax revenue into GDP had for many countries increased at a very fast pace, especially before the new millennium (see Tanzi, 2011a, table 4.1, p. 95). During these years, public debt had been increasingly used to finance higher levels of public spending, in spite of the increases in tax levels. Therefore, higher taxes and increased public borrowing fed the fast-rising levels of public spending as shares of the countries' GDPs. Because of the move to become members of the EMU and because of various dubious operations that are described in a different chapter, the period between 1995 and 2005 was associated with statistics that might have appeared to be but were not consistent with fiscal sustainability, as claimed by Mauro *et al.* in a recent study (2013).

In those years, the economic activities of many countries were undergoing a period of intense globalization, because of the liberal trade and especially because of financial policies that were being introduced. The globalization was creating increasing difficulties for tax administrations in the collection of taxes, especially when the tax rates were high. Tax evasion connected with global activities started to attract increasing attention, whereas in the past tax evasion had been mainly a domestic phenomenon, often connected with the overstating of expenses and underground or non reported economic activities. At the same time, the high levels reached by many countries' tax revenues were creating growing political opposition by citizens. These developments were making it progressively more difficult for governments to keep increasing the level of taxation in order to finance their expenditures, which in many countries were already very high. However, public spending continued to rise.

Strong political and also administrative pressures had been building up in several countries, especially in the decade of the 1990s, to begin to lower the levels of taxes. For example the Berlusconi government, which had won the election in Italy in 2001, had, during the electoral campaign, promised to immediately introduce a tax reform that would reduce the tax burden of Italy by several percentage points of GDP. That government would not be able to deliver on this promise, but not for lack of intent. The Bush administration in the United States sharply reduced taxes, in spite of having to fight two wars and of having a growing fiscal deficit. In those years flat-rate taxes became popular and were introduced in some countries in Eastern Europe.

Opposition to higher taxes has remained strong among the American population, in spite of the relatively low tax level in the USA and among the populations of other countries. It continues to be strong in several European countries. For example the tax increases in Italy and in France by the governments in power in the second part of 2012 cost those governments a lot of popularity. By the decade of the 2000s, these movements had brought about a stop in the growth of tax levels in most countries (see Tanzi, *ibid.*). Thus further increases in public spending could be financed only by increased public debt.

For the three largest EMU countries, over the 20 years 1977–97 before the EMU was created the shares of public debt into GDP had increased by the following percentages: in Germany from 26.8 percent to 65.2 percent; in France from 20.1 percent to 64.2 percent; and in Italy from 56.4 percent to 103.3 percent. The continuation of these trends would inevitably lead to future difficulties.

As already mentioned, for a few years *after* 1997, when the Maastricht treaty was signed, the fiscal situation, as measured by the reported fiscal deficits, improved. Member countries tried to live, at least formally, within the constraints of the fiscal rules to which they had prescribed. However, as shown earlier, there is evidence, from various sources also already reported, that some of such improvements were more apparent than real. Various tricks were used to report better official data.

A few years later, several countries, including France and Germany, broke the 3 percent fiscal limit rule on their deficits, blaming the weakening of their economies. The fiscal deficit rule was amended to make it more flexible and to accommodate cyclical variations. The structural deficit was given a larger role than the actual deficit. Public spending soon resumed its fast rate of growth in many of the countries, and in some it reached high levels that were difficult to finance. These difficulties would be accentuated and would become obvious at the time of the financial crisis.

However, when the crisis came, much of public attention in the European countries would be diverted from the difficulties of financing the high level that public spending had reached in previous years to that of saving the euro. Some attributed the high interest rates that came to prevail in several countries where the public accounts were under stress to the irrational behavior of creditors, or to the action of speculators.

A final comment is due on the policies followed by the EMU countries in the decade before the crisis. Some Catholics, among others, believe that persistent prayers can occasionally produce miracles. Strong incentives can do the same now and then in the economic area. The period between around 2000 and 2007 looks very much like a miracle for the EMU countries. Almost magically the large differences in interest rates, in fiscal deficits, and in some other variables seemed to vanish, rather like snow under a strong sun. Some of these differences would reappear, starting in 2008. A doubt remains whether they had actually been eliminated, or, rather, had been buried under a fog of complexity, inaccurate or even dishonest reporting, and so on.

# 8
# Fiscal Policy During the Recent Crisis

The creation of the European Monetary Union had given, at least in a statistical sense, large, additional fiscal space to the member countries, by sharply lowering the interest rates they had been paying on their public debt. This lowering of interest rates was in part more apparent than real, because it was due to the fall in nominal interest rates caused by the fall in the inflation rates. The real interest rates had fallen much less than the nominal rates. For several countries, including Belgium, Greece, and Italy, the lowering of the nominal rates on their public debt had reduced their share of GDP by several points. For example, from 1995 to 2003 the interest payment on the public debt had fallen in Belgium from 8.9 percent to 5.3 percent, in Greece from 11.3 percent to 5.0 percent, and in Italy from 11.5 percent to 5.1 percent. Because of these reductions, the countries' governments must have felt suddenly richer. They must have believed that their fiscal policy had become far more sustainable. Unfortunately, the fiscal space so created was not used to reduce the public debt, as the countries might have been expected to do. In several countries the acquired fiscal space was instead used to increase public spending.

The bubbles that started developing in some countries, and especially the USA, in the early years of the new millennium, through the artificial but not permanent raising of some countries' tax revenue and perhaps even their growth rates, gave the impression, to policymakers and other economic observers, that the economic and fiscal developments in those years were healthier than they actually were. They may have also been affected by the fiscal illusion created by the accounting tricks used. Thus the bubble-related tax revenue had the same effect on some countries as had the savings in interest payments when the EMU came into existence. Many economists in those years had come to believe that the "new normal" was a world without business cycles, because the *maestros* running the central banks had learned how to eliminate them through their wise use of monetary policy. See Woodward (2005) and Greenspan (2007).

By comparison, the inflated economic performances in those bubble years would make the years after 2008 look worse than they actually were. The financial crisis of 2008–09, and the Great Recession that accompanied and followed it, which according to various estimates reduced the levels of GDPs by several percentage points below their presumed *potentials*, exposed the full, and in some sense more accurate, permanent fiscal situations. They also created the controversy of whether a Keynesian solution could not come to the rescue of the countries' economies, and bring the actual GDPs closer to their potential GDPs estimated on the basis of the pre-crisis years. Some economists have estimated the potential GDP of the United States to be at least 7 per cent of GDP higher than the actual, current (2012) GDP. In other countries the percentage difference between their potential and the actual GDPs has been estimated to be at least as high as or higher than in the USA. It also generated the debate of whether governments should pursue *austerity* or *growth,* assuming, as some did, that the countries' governments had the luxury of making that choice.

Some American economists, including Paul Krugman, Larry Summers, Christina Romer, and others, came down flatly on the side of "growth," by which they meant a continuation of policies associated with large fiscal deficits, or even with a sustained increase in current public spending, until unemployment fell to pre-recession level. They argued that particular types of public spending, as for example for infrastructure or education, would contribute to faster growth rates and, through the higher growth, would help reduce the fiscal imbalances. They seem to have no doubts that such a fiscal policy would not affect the country's fiscal sustainability.

Other economists, including Edmund Phelps, Kenneth Rogoff, Alberto Alesina, and some others, have argued that in the present circumstances a growth strategy based on fiscal expansion, rather than on fundamental structural reforms that would not require additional public spending, was not a realistic option, given the fiscal conditions of many countries. They are convinced that such a strategy would likely be counterproductive and probably unsustainable over the medium or long run. Below, we discuss briefly this important and controversial question of *growth versus austerity*. It should be added that this debate involved all the countries in difficulty, and not just the US or the members of the EMU. In Italy the government that had been presided by Mario Monti was accused of having introduced too much "austerity," especially by increasing the already very high tax burden, while paying much less attention to growth. As a consequence Monti received little support in the elections. Other European governments had to deal with similar criticisms and major street demonstrations.

As we maintained earlier, if a recession is one of the traditional business cycle variety, one due to the "weakening of animal spirits" on the part of consumers and investors; and if the initial fiscal conditions of a country are good and sustainable, then many, though perhaps not all, economists, would support policies aimed at strengthening aggregate demand, through a *temporary* fiscal expansion. However, let us assume that the recession is not one of the traditional kind associated with the weakening of animal spirits (spirits that would be expected to spontaneously reverse themselves in countries that did not have significant bubbles). Rather it is a crisis associated with major and policy-induced distortions in the use of resources, which had generated bubbles and *unsustainable* current account deficits and other imbalances that had made the bursting of the bubbles almost inevitable at some point in the future.

Whether originating from excessive monetary expansion or from excessive savings on the part of China and some other countries, savings that were channeled to and invested in the bubble countries, the bubbles would normally be concentrated in one or several large sectors of the economy, which would grow disproportionately. Historical experience from several countries indicates that the bubbles are often concentrated in the construction and related sectors. The short-run increase in the prices of the outputs, produced by the bubble sectors, make these investments look profitable and efficient at the time when they are made. They make consumers feel richer. This was the situation that developed in many countries in the years before 2007–08.

The incentives that drove the behavior of financial market operators, the increasing complexity in the financial market that presumably spread risks, the inefficient regulations, and also the lack of adequate statistical information on what was going on, aided also by some acts of corruption and of misleading information on the part of some market participants, all contributed to the economic developments that created the bubbles. (See among many recent books on the subject Sinn, 2010; Rajan, 2010; Lewis, 2010; Admati and Hellwig, 2013; and others.)

In the period before the so-called Great Recession, the bubbles, which were largely financed by expansionary monetary policy and by *cheap,* and often *foreign* loans, rather than by domestic savings, had been increasingly evident in sectors such as housing and, more broadly, construction and sectors in various ways associated with the construction industry; in finance; in the auto industry; and in some other areas. These sectors were producing outputs that would be considered excessive after the crisis erupted. After the crisis the value of these outputs (say houses) would fall sharply. Some of this output produced would be left unsold. This raises questions about how genuine the growth rates during the bubble years had been. It also raises the question of whether the estimated pre-recession growth rates should not be revised downward, *ex post* in order to reflect the true value of what had been produced in those years.

Bubbles and the value of what they produce are normally accompanied by large imbalances in the external sector, especially when the financial market is global and the economies are open, so that much cross-countries capital movement can take place. This had been the case in the pre-bubble years, particularly for some countries, within the European Monetary Union. Because of common causes, bubbles may affect several countries at the same time, thus creating major cross-countries spillover effects, which contribute to the difficulties in coordinating global policies.

The dangers connected with these situations are, first, that governments that find it easy to borrow cheaply, especially from foreign sources, will be tempted to over-borrow. Second, that particular private activities within countries may tend to over-borrow if credit is cheap and if existing regulations, especially on banks, are not adequate. Add to this the often limited aggregate, statistical information available on what is going on, the complexity of some of the financial undertaking, plus perhaps a belief that the private market generally works efficiently, and that governments cannot go broke, and you have all the elements that can contribute to a financial crisis.

A financial crisis that creates great difficulties for banks will almost inevitably force governments to intervene, thus contributing to the fiscal problems. There are lots of examples from many countries that point to this almost inevitable conclusion. It was the US experience and that of several countries within the EMU. Thus financial liberalization and the creation of a global financial market, that had had the potential to improve the allocation of resources on a worldwide basis, also created the potential to create major financial instability in the world. Whether the potential advantages of financial liberalization exceed the potential costs is an issue that will not be pursued here.

In a country's economy, a crisis that does not have its origin in the weakening of animal spirits – a weakening that, for often unexplained psychological reasons, can occur in a country in which the allocation of resources has been broadly correct – but rather originates from a pre-crisis major misallocation of financial and real resources, including workers, presents the authorities of the affected country with particular problems. For example, as mentioned earlier, the existence of the bubbles is likely to have inflated the country's pre-crisis growth rate, as well as the country's tax revenue, because of the economic activities and the windfall taxes that the bubble sectors have generated.

Some recent literature has shown empirically the rather obvious point that the *structure* of the national income, as distinguished from its *level*, can influence tax revenue, because some sectors are greater contributors to revenue than other sectors (see, for example, Sancak *et al.*, 2010). These developments can easily create the perception that, before the crisis, the economic and the fiscal situations were sounder than they actually were. This was the case in several European countries and in the United States, before the financial crisis (see Tanzi, 2012b, for some elaboration of this point). As a consequence, it becomes more difficult to determine correctly the true magnitude of some important variables, and especially the "structural deficit" and the "potential income," statistics that are needed to determine the size of a "required" fiscal expansion, or of a fiscal correction (see also Tanzi, 2011b).

Besides reducing the countries' saving rates (by increasing consumer spending as a consequence of perceived, large, and often unrealized capital gains on assets, including houses), the pre-crisis bubbles had created excess supplies of some products and activities (houses, shopping centers, equipments and supplies for furnishing new houses, real estate agencies, cars and car dealerships, some specialized financial services, retail outlets, etc.). It had also generated major asset-price effects, by creating capital gains connected with the prices of houses and some other assets. These asset-prices effects have been estimated to be in trillions of dollars in the United States. For example, according to Fed statistics, the US household wealth, that had been $ 67.4 trillion before the recession, fell to $51.4 trillion in early 2009.

After the bursting of the bubbles, some durable physical goods and some services remained in excess supply for extended periods because they could not be eliminated quickly. The pre-crisis positive asset-price effects on wealth reversed themselves, because of the fall in the prices of the assets. This reversal made millions of people poorer, including especially those who lost their houses, because they could not – or, in the USA in some cases, they did not want to – continue servicing their mortgages. The large capital gains that had been created before the financial crisis became large post-crisis capital losses. Many newly built houses and commercial buildings remained empty, pushing down the value of the total housing stock (that included that of old houses) and that of commercial buildings.

In the United States, Spain, Ireland, Portugal, and to a lesser extent in some other countries, the excess supply of houses, when the bubble burst, was enormous. Millions of newly built houses remained unsold and empty. Some were vandalized, further reducing their values. In many cases, the market value of the houses fell below the value of the mortgages that had allowed their owners to buy the houses. Millions of workers that had been engaged in activities related to the construction industry (as real estate agents or as financial operators) lost their jobs. Because of the fall in personal wealth, and the associated fall in income and consumption, many retail shops were forced to close, contributing to the rise in unemployment, even in countries such as Italy that had not been initially affected by the sub-prime crisis. Newly produced cars remained unsold, thus reducing the value not only of new cars but also that of the total existing stock of used cars, which depends on the price of new ones.

According to an estimate, made by Moody's Analytics, based on Census and Bureau of Labor statistics data, since 2006, US homeowners have lost an average real value of $122 000 per household, most of it due to falling house prices. The average home equity per homeowner, in 2011 prices, fell to the 1968 level. The estimate was reported by the *New York Times* on 8 April 2012 (see "The Collapse of Home Equity"). This loss occurred at the same time when, according to the latest IMF data, the US *gross* public debt rose from 66.6 percent to 107.2 percent of GDP, creating enormous additional future tax liabilities for American households. These data ignore the huge liabilities, vis-à-vis workers, associated with current pensions systems and health benefits. These effects are not likely to disappear for years to come. They have already led to the bankruptcies of several American cities. In the UK there were similar trends but they were, perhaps, also associated with developments in the financial market that saw a significant expansion in employment and profits followed by a large contraction. The UK has also been experiencing a sharp rise in its gross public debt, from 43.3 percent of GDP in 2006 to 88.7 percent of GDP in 2012. This increase is expected to continue for several years to come in spite of the government desire to reduce the fiscal deficit. It is expected to continue to increase significantly for the next few years. As a consequence of this expected development, on 22 February 2013, Moody removed the AAA rating for the UK.

The excesses in the supply of some goods and services must also have had some, *downward,* influence on the indices that are used to measure inflationary trends, thus contributing to the fear, expressed by some observers, especially at the beginning of the crisis, about the potential danger of deflation. These fears have been less frequently expressed in more recent times, because there has been little evidence of deflation. On the contrary, recent evidence indicates some significant increases in inflationary expectations, or in current prices, in at least some countries, including the UK and Italy. Housing and, to a lesser extent, cars contribute a significant share of the total costs that official indexes use to estimate inflationary pressures therefore the fall in their prices influences in a downward direction the price indexes. The fear of deflation had led some economists to press harder for expansionary monetary policies and for central banks to increase their balance sheets by more than they would have done. Quantitative easing policies and other similar policies were in part justified by these fears, at least in the early years of the crisis.

The economic crisis that followed the bursting of the bubbles inevitably reduced the demand for workers, leading to higher unemployment, and for longer periods of time, than had normally been the case in past recessions, especially among the workers employed in sectors most affected by the bursting bubbles. Millions of these workers had been occupied producing new houses or new constructions or the materials and the equipments that would fill the houses, or selling the houses. Many more workers had been busy processing and selling the mortgages to buy the new houses. Facing the difficulties in finding new jobs, some of these workers are likely to drop out of the labor force, reducing the future number of workers actively looking for work.

The bursting of the bubbles could not fail to have major consequences for fiscal policy. A first consequence was that a *discretionary* fiscal expansion was likely to have less of an impact on the economy than would be the case when a recession is of a more traditional type. The reason is that it will take more time for the unemployed resources to be fully redeployed, often in sectors that are *different from* those where they had been employed before the crisis and in which they had acquired expertise. They will have to move from the activities that had closed down to newly created activities. This will take time and money. Just think of the workers who had lost their jobs in the housing or the financial sectors, and in specific locations, and who need to move to new jobs created by the governments' fiscal stimulus programs, perhaps producing new energy. These new sectors will require skills that the workers do not have, and will often be located in different geographical areas.

This means that the countries that experienced the recessions are likely to perform at what may appear to be less than full capacity for a time that may seem too long. It also means that, during this period, a period that might extend over several years, economic growth will be lower than before the crisis, and unemployment will be higher. (See on this also the papers by Phelps, 2010, and by Zoega, 2010.) By reducing tax revenue and by increasing some spending (as for unemployment or for earlier retirement) this low economic activity will inevitably also affect negatively the fiscal accounts, which will remain precarious and will continue to be a cause for concern. Public debts as shares of GDPs will keep rising, implying rising future servicing costs for governments and higher future taxes for the citizens. The rise in public debt will of course also depend on the interest rates that governments pay when they borrow money which are likely to go up. A return of interest rates to historical levels could easily add a trillion dollars to the yearly fiscal deficit of the US after a few years.

A second consequence is that a discretionary fiscal expansion is not likely to help the economy much, especially if its immediate and medium-run effect is, or might be, to increase, at least in the short run, fiscal deficits, interest rates, and public debt; and if, as is likely, the reallocation of resources across sectors of the economy faces inevitable and significant friction, high costs, and productivity losses. Recall that the excess supplies and the unemployed resources have been highly concentrated in some geographical areas and in some sectors of the economy. They are not spread widely and evenly, as one would expect to be more the case in traditional, Keynesian recessions. Increases in interest rates, and continued high unemployment, have been common features, since the beginning of the crisis, in various countries. These developments should not have surprised the policymakers and the economists.

A third consequence, and one that merits far more attention than it has received in the literature that deals with macroeconomic fiscal policy, is that large fiscal deficits and rising public debts are not ignored by economic operators. They are likely to create inevitable, and at times potentially damaging, *psychological* reactions on the part of investors (both domestic and foreign) and on the part of consumers. The reason is that when fiscal deficits and public debts reach high levels they increase concerns about the long-run consequences and the sustainability of the current fiscal policies, and also the implications of future failures or future policies. These concerns are not limited to potential "Ricardian equivalence" reactions that have attracted the attention of academic economists.

As the levels of the fiscal deficits and of the public debts increase, a decreasing number of individuals are likely to believe the optimistic version of expansionary Keynesian fiscal policy that some economists have been pushing. Is the so-called troika (the EU, the ECB and the IMF) wrong in asking Greece, and other countries asking for financial assistance to spend less, given their fiscal conditions? Would foreign or domestic investments in these countries increase if their governments announced that they would follow the advice of some economists and start spending more? One must remain skeptical about these claims.

The role of the media, in creating both positive and negative psychological reactions to growing public debts and high fiscal deficits, has become more important than it might have been in the past, when there were no blogs, and the news that individuals received was much more limited. Today individuals are continually bombarded by information. Economic news is reported daily by various means of communication, and bad news attracts more attention from the media than good news. It is unlikely that reports about higher fiscal deficits and growing public debts would make people anticipate more prosperous times, as some economists may believe, when the levels reached by these variables have already become high.

The negative psychological reactions to growing public debts are likely to encourage many investors, who might have the capacity to make economic decisions, to wait before they commit resources to new real investments, or before they hire new workers, even when such investors have the financial means to do so. These psychological reactions also encourage consumers who have the needed liquidity to postpone some consumption (cars, houses and major appliances) that can be postponed. These psychological reactions are likely to reduce the expected impact on economic activity of so-called expansionary fiscal and monetary policies, or even to reverse it.

An unusual aspect of the recent economic slowdown has been the large amounts of financial resources that enterprises have had available, especially in the US, but that have not been invested in real activities or used to hire new workers. In the USA at the end of 2012 this money was being used to increase the distribution of dividends, in anticipation of likely higher taxes in the future. Large amounts of these resources have been parked in the banks or in public securities with short maturity or with the Fed, as reserves, where they have been collecting trivial returns.

It has been widely reported that in 2012, US companies had on hand in cash somewhere around $2 *trillion* that were not being used either for making investments or for hiring workers. The *value of waiting* in making these decisions had definitely risen, and investors and consumers had become more careful in their spending decisions. Both investors and consumers must worry about the sustainability of the current fiscal policies, and about future policies, fearing that the large fiscal imbalances will, in time, lead to higher taxes, or to lower spending on programs that benefits them. If the situation became truly precarious, the fiscal imbalances could even lead to sovereign defaults, at least in some countries. In these circumstances, waiting to make economic decisions, or in some cases even taking the money out of the countries and to safer places, becomes a natural and highly rational course of action, or of inaction, on the part of individuals and enterprises. These latter actions have been going on in some European countries and the USA has benefited by remaining one of the safer places yet where to place one's money.

An interesting article by Gillian Tett in the *Financial Times* (22 September 2012, p. 20) reported on a survey conducted at Duke University in which 887 chief financial officers of large companies were asked how they might respond to falling interest rates. An overwhelming proportion, over 90 percent, responded that falls in interest rates, even by one or even two percentage points, would have no impact on their investing or hiring decisions. Clearly the value of waiting is so high, because of worries about future developments, that neither a monetary expansion that reduces interest rates nor, likely, a fiscal expansion would make a positive difference and might even be counterproductive. Different policies would be needed to lower the *value of waiting*. In countries with smaller economies than the United States and with greater immediate concerns about the fiscal situation, individuals and enterprises with available balances may prefer not to wait but to exit, leading to capital flight, as has been happening in some European countries. If the assets that they own are in government bonds, the attempt to sell the bonds inevitably leads to the fall in their value and the increase in the interest rate for the government to replace the borrowing. This in turn can affect the cost of capital in the private sector, mainly for longer-maturity loans that are more sensitive to potential risks. We shall come back to this issue.

If fiscal deficits remained high, while economic growth remained low, which is a realistic scenario under present conditions in several countries, the already high share of public debt into GDP, which exists in many countries, would keep rising, as it has been rising rapidly so far in the US, the UK, Japan and several European countries. This increase would inevitably attract more media attention and more negative comments by an increasing number of economists and financial operators, comments that would reinforce the existing negative psychological reactions to the precarious fiscal situation mentioned earlier.

Recent research by various economists, some of which has been mentioned earlier, has shown that while the short-run effect on economic activity of higher public debt might be positive when the ratio of public debt to GDP is still low, it becomes negative when the ratio becomes high and when it begins to have an impact on interest rates or, perhaps, on the psychology of individuals. The reason is the rather obvious one that, at high levels of debt-to-GDP ratios (levels that may differ from country to country, or even from period to period), concerns for fiscal sustainability are likely to grow. This makes investors less inclined to sink their money in fixed investments in which the danger may not be one of earning a lower rate of return, but one of losing the money that has been invested. Even when default is not immediately on the cards, future high taxes or future high inflation and higher interest rates may become major concerns. As mentioned, this may encourage some economic operators to "vote with their feet" by taking their money to safer countries if such countries are still available.

The above discussion has obvious implications for the size of the multipliers that may accompany a fiscal expansion, an issue that has recently attracted a lot of attention. In recent and earlier years several authors have attempted to estimate the size of the multipliers that play such a large role in Keynesian economics. They have tried to answer the question: if a government increases public spending by one, what will be the final impact of that increase on the economy? Keynesian economics predicts that the impact will be greater than the initial additional spending and in some circumstances much greater than the initial spending. The magnitude of the increase is assumed to depend on the marginal propensity to consume of individuals and the openness of the economy. The higher the propensity to consume and the closer the economy, the greater will be the multiplier. The theory assumes that the higher private incomes that are created by the fiscal expansion will *not* end up trapped in the balance of some investors or consumers who will not use them and that the financing of the money that the government spends does not have a negative direct effect on consumption or investment. That is, the immediate, higher fiscal deficits will not have negative psychological or other repercussions on economic operators, or scare them into taking the capital out of the country. Those who receive the additional income must have faith in the power of Keynesian fiscal policies.

It should be recognized that Keynesian multipliers reflect purely *mechanical* relations and that, as in all mechanical relations, the ratio between the initial effort (say the higher public spending) and the final result (say the effect on the economy) will depend on various real-world circumstances, which may vary from case to case and not depend just on the unused capacity in the economy.

In some ways the problem in determining the size of multipliers is similar to that of trying to measure how many miles per gallon of gasoline a car can travel. In a windless day, on a well-paved flat road, and with well-inflated tires, when a car encounters little resistance, one will get one answer. However, if the car is moving in the middle of a storm, with strong headwinds, on a mountain road, and perhaps with tires that are not well inflated, the relation between gasoline used and distance covered could change dramatically. High public debt and anxiety about the future can play the part of high and contrary winds, or of a road that is not flat.

There is likely to exist an inverse relation between the level reached by the public debt in a country and the size of the multiplier in that country. The higher is the debt, at the time when a fiscal stimulus package is introduced the lower is likely to be the multiplier. Multipliers can even become negative under given circumstances, when the "spread" on borrowing has become very high and this encourages investors to take their money abroad. Therefore, it would seem to be a waste of valuable time, on the part of economists, to attempt to measure Keynesian multipliers in the circumstances that have prevailed in many countries since 2008, as some have attempted to do. It is no surprise that different economists have produced highly differing estimates and that they have reached different conclusions (see, inter alia, Golinelli and Momigliano, 2008; Egers, 2013; Giavazzi, 2010; Blanchard and Leigh, 2012; DeLong and Summers, 2012; Ilzetzki *et al.*, 2013; Chinn, 2012; and Corsetti, 2012).

It is interesting that the size of the multipliers that the researchers estimate often reflects the a priori views of the researchers on the power of fiscal policy. It is obviously difficult or impossible in empirical work to separate the effect of a fiscal expansion when so much else (changing monetary policy, changes in the tax structure, etc.) is going on. Technical sophistication on the part of those who carry out this work cannot make the results more credible. Applying the law of torture to the data can often produce the results that one wishes to produce.

In conclusion, it would truly require a "suspension of disbelief," or total irrationality on the part of individuals, to continue to assume that developments in the fiscal accounts that are likely to lead to significantly higher public debt when the debt position is already high will have no negative impacts (but only a positive one) on investors' propensity to invest and on individuals' propensity to consume. It is naive to assume that developments would have only positive effects, through significant and positive multipliers, that would make the economies grow fast enough to prevent the growth of the debt/GDP ratio as argued in the recent paper by DeLong and Summers. The economists and politicians who keep calling for fiscal expansion, in the current precarious fiscal circumstances of many countries, ignore, or minimize, the potential, but likely negative, reactions that the policies that they recommend could have.

There are several reasons to assume that, especially when a recession is due to the bursting of bubbles, as was the Great Recession in several countries and especially in the US, the goal of discretionary fiscal policy, *in the short run*, might have to change, from the traditional one of sustaining aggregate demand to, perhaps, that of protecting, where necessary, through temporary public assistance, the most vulnerable citizens – those that are negatively and significantly affected directly by the crisis and that do not have assets or families to help them in the short run. This temporary assistance might be provided while exit strategies from the high public debts and the large fiscal deficits that must include structural reforms are being considered. The protective goal suggested just above is obviously different from the traditional one associated with Keynesian policies. It is a goal that can and should be limited in time, to ensure that it does not add permanently to public spending.

The above discussion implies that it may not be a wise policy for countries' governments to wait until the economic situation returns to "normal," whatever that means, before beginning to introduce policies aimed at *reducing* the size of the fiscal deficits and at containing the rise in the level of public debt, as some economists continue to maintain. For the medium run, the so-called "new normal" is likely to be an economic situation with lower growth and higher unemployment than before the crisis. This situation may not change as long as the fiscal accounts are not brought under control, even if it must be recognized that the action of bringing the fiscal situation under better control may, temporarily, have some unwanted, negative effect on a country's economic activity and possibly on its employment. These negative short-run effects are now visible in some countries, such as Italy, Portugal, and the UK (see also Cottarelli and Jaramillo, 2012, on this point). Allowing the fiscal deficits to remain high, or even to increase, as some economists recommend, in the hope that this will promote growth, would likely do little to change this reality. However, it would make the longer-run situation worse, by increasing the ratio of public debt to GDP, and perhaps also by reducing the potency of monetary expansion.

There are some other issues more connected with the long-run, traditional, Keynesian theory of fiscal policy, than with the immediate situation, that may be worth mentioning briefly. They are related to what some have defined the political, rather than the technical, power of economic ideas (see Hall, 1989). Some of the political power of the Keynesian way of looking at the economic situation may have contributed to the continuous increase in the share of public spending in the economy. This influence became obvious over recent decades, especially after World War Two when public spending and public debt grew considerably in many countries, often in the belief that fiscal deficits, by contributing to aggregate demand, which was assumed to be consistently, or often, deficient, promoted economic growth, even in normal times.

The growth of the fiscal variables, in recent decades in most advanced countries, was not caused by major wars, as it often had been in the past or by major depressions. It occurred in normal, peaceful, and prosperous periods. It reflected the social preferences on the part of the countries' citizens for a growing economic role of the state (see Tanzi, 2011a). It perhaps reflected also the countries' ability in earlier years to finance the extra spending easily, first with higher taxes and then, when the increase in tax revenues was no longer sufficient, with public debt. Globalization may have facilitated the debt financing for some countries, because it gave access to other countries' excess balances. However, globalization may in time have reduced the facility with which governments had raised taxes when the economies had been less open (see Tanzi 2011a). The increasingly ambitious economic role that was demanded from the state required a lot of additional government spending. That spending, at some point, became too large to sustain easily. It started to create economic difficulties for governments that would grow in intensity in an increasing number of countries.

The first, longer-run, problems connected with the Keynesian ideology could be called those of "policy asymmetry." A basic, implicit assumption, made by supporters of countercyclical fiscal policy, is that the policymakers who make the policy decisions (a) do not have political or personal biases; (b) have the information and the power to change the fiscal variables, in both directions, when necessary; and (c) when they make mistakes, make random rather than systematic ones. Therefore, the policymakers were assumed to be as ready to pursue expansionary fiscal policies, and as capable in their pursuit, when these policies were needed, as they would be to pursue restrictive fiscal actions. In other words, countercyclical policy was assumed to be symmetric in its effect on public spending over the long run.

However, much evidence over the years from many countries indicates that, in the real world, policymakers often reflect a clear asymmetry, or a bias, in the pursuit of countercyclical fiscal policy. The policymakers, who make the relevant decisions, are often far more favorably disposed to pursue fiscal policies that are expansionary than ones that are restrictive. They seem to have far more freedom and political interest in *increasing* public spending, and perhaps in *reducing* taxes, than in doing the opposite. This bias was encouraged and defended, over the years, by economists who believed that the market has many failures that government can correct with its fiscal actions so that higher spending is almost always beneficial. They also believed that countries grow faster, even in normal times, when their economies are being propelled by fiscal deficits.

Two other long-run asymmetries that may have led to similar results could be called "bureaucratic asymmetries" and "citizens' asymmetries."

The *bureaucratic asymmetry* has two facets. One is the role that the heads of government offices or agencies (the high-level bureaucrats) play in pushing for the expansions of their budgets and for the power of their offices. A reason for this behavior is that the importance and power of these individuals, and, perhaps, even their compensation, often depend on the size of the budgets of their offices. This role that bureaucracies may play in the growth of public spending received considerable academic attention in recent decades, especially in the literature on "public choice." (See, for descriptions of this bureaucratic asymmetry, Niskanen, 1971; Peacock, 1992; Mueller, 2003.)

The other aspect is that higher public expenditure is often associated with more public sector jobs and, especially, with better working conditions for government employees, including safer jobs, higher salaries, longer vacations, more generous retirement pensions, and other benefits. In many countries public employees constitute a powerful lobby that favors, and that benefits from, higher public spending. It is no coincidence that the European countries that got into fiscal difficulties after 2007 had, in the years before the crisis, significantly increased the benefits of their public employees, resulting in higher, and at times much higher, public–private wage differentials, which, in turn, through the demonstration effect, may have contributed to higher private sector wages (see Giordano *et al.*, 2011; Lamo *et al.*, 2011).

When fiscal retrenchment becomes unavoidable, because of a fiscal crisis, or because of difficulty in continuing to get access to reasonably priced debt by the governments, the public employees, because of their past generous treatment, may be among the first to be singled out for benefit reductions by the governments' restrictive policies. For example, the governments of Greece, Ireland, Italy, Portugal, and other countries have been trying to reduce the benefits to public sector employees in the recent crisis years. These governments have tried to reduce salaries, pension rights, and the number of public sector employees. It is natural that the employees so affected have a strong incentive to try to neutralize these policies in various ways. They can do it explicitly, with strikes or work slowdowns; or in more subtle ways, through various kinds of passive resistance, including working strictly to the rules and taking full advantage of sick leaves.

Passarelli and Tabellini (2013) have recently theorized that "political unrest is motivated by emotions" and that when changes in policies are seen as unfair by some groups they will get organized and will try to stop the changes. They provide several recent examples where political unrest has stopped needed reforms. Thus the same power of public sector unions, that over the years had pushed for benefit increases, can prevent the more rapid reduction in those benefits and can try to shift the cost of the adjustment onto other groups, perhaps pensioners or welfare recipients, or onto the educational and public health sectors. The best recent examples have come from Greece, Portugal, and Spain, where there has been a tug of war between the governments and the public employees who have fought hard to neutralize the policies that would have reduced their benefits or their numbers.

In the case of *citizens' or voters' asymmetries* which is related to the above, because fiscal policy is often focused on specific subsectors of the population (pensioners, schoolteachers, specific categories of taxpayers, etc.), more than on the populace in general, those who will be more negatively affected by the fiscal retrenchments are likely to be the ones who will react more forcefully, either with accusations of unfairness or with other more direct forms of resistance. It is rarely that the effects of either lax fiscal policies or restrictive ones are *proportionally or broadly spread* throughout the whole population. Their impact is almost always selective and more focused on particular classes or groups of citizens. This gives the groups most affected a stronger incentive to organize, both in favor of higher benefits, in normal times, or against spending cuts, in bad times; or against higher taxes that affect them. Sometimes the organization tends to be political and directed at supporting particular candidates in the next elections, as happened in the United States in 2012. In the US the term "class warfare" has been used to try to prevent any tax increases on the super-rich, individuals who have benefited from unusually low tax rates in recent years (see Tanzi, 2012c).

These likely reactions have contributed, over the years, to the asymmetry in the use of fiscal policy and to the growth of public spending and public debt, as shares of GDPs, in many of the countries now facing fiscal difficulties. These reactions must be combined with or may even have contributed to the long-run trend toward higher spending described by *a law of growing public spending* that will be outlined in a later chapter.

# 9
# Fiscal Policy and the Fiction of Fungible Labor

In this chapter we discuss some reasons why unemployment rates tend to remain high for a long time after the bursting of bubbles and why fiscal stimulus packages often tend to be disappointing in terms of job creation. This has clearly been the case in the most recent years in the countries that have experienced the Great Recession. The reason is mainly that labor is much less fungible than Keynesian fiscal policy has assumed it to be and that workers find it much more difficult to change jobs than assumed by Keynesian economics. Furthermore, it can be theorized that the difficulties described in this chapter are likely to grow as the countries' economies become more advanced and complex.

As countries become richer and as their economies become more developed, to operate well they require more human capital, and especially more human capital of a *specialized* kind. In fact, economic development means largely the use of new technologies and the progressive acquisition of new, useful skills by a growing portion of a country's population to use those technologies. This is what is called the acquisition of human capital, the capital that is the most important determinant of a country's level of development.

As development economics has shown, there is a high correlation between economic development on one hand and the amount of human capital that a country possesses on the other. The differences in workers' compensation, between low-skill activities that require little human capital, and pay low or minimum wages, and those that require a lot of training, education, and talent, and that pay higher wages, reflect, to a large extent, the importance of human capital and the way that that capital is distributed among the working population.

In economies that grow smoothly, and that have flexible labor markets and good educational and training systems, the labor force adjusts, automatically and continually, in order to acquire the skills that the market activities require. In turn, given the relative scarcity of useful skills, the market determines the differences in wages and salaries among the workers. In a well-working economy, these differences reflect broadly the abundance of the different skills available.

To a large extent, *in a well-working labor market*, the Gini coefficient (measured before the payment of taxes), which indicates the distribution of income among those who receive labor income, is an indication of the extent of the differentiation in skills and in specialization that exists among the individuals that comprise the labor force of a country. It follows that, as workers become progressively more specialized in the specific jobs that they do, they become progressively less interchangeable, or fungible, among themselves and across jobs. A brain surgeon is not interchangeable with a carpenter, or a taxi-driver with a commercial pilot.

When major bubbles develop in some sectors (finance, housing and related activities, and others), and they start generating higher demand and higher incomes for the workers who work in those sectors, they will attract new workers to them. Over the years, while the bubbles persist, more people will acquire the skills demanded in those sectors. The longer an economy experiences the existence of bubbles (i.e. overexpansion) in particular sectors, and the more important are those sectors, the larger will be the number of workers who will have incentives to acquire the required skills and to gravitate toward those sectors. Employment and incomes will consequently grow at a faster pace in the bubble sectors.

Just think of the attraction that the financial market created for individuals who graduated from business schools in recent decades. As the financial market grew in importance in the economy of some countries, the business schools started attracting an increasing numbers of students who in the past would have gone to different schools and into different specializations. The new students acquired the skills that were most in demand in the financial sector and that would allow them to earn the high incomes that had come to characterize that sector. Even some "rocket scientists," who had acquired mathematical skills that could be used to earn higher incomes in the financial market than in the space industry, were attracted to it. In the United States, for example, the share of total US corporate profits that was generated by the financial sector went from around 5 percent to around 40 percent over the postwar period. This change, and the very high incomes that some individuals were reported to receive in that sector, made the financial market a large magnet for graduates from business schools. A similar phenomenon, though at lower income levels, happened in the housing sector and in the many activities connected with the broadly defined construction sector. The same may have been happening recently in the energy sector.

When, around 2007, the bubble burst in the housing, financial, and related sectors, many of the workers in those sectors lost their jobs. However, the skills that they had acquired, to operate efficiently in those sectors, were not easily usable in other sectors. Even when the workers that lost their jobs could get jobs in other sectors of the economy, they would not be able to get incomes close to those that they had been receiving in the jobs that they had lost. They were thus reluctant to accept the available jobs and willing to remain unemployed longer in the hope of reentering the labor force at or near the income levels they had enjoyed before the bubbles burst. If they were older workers, close to retirement, and had accumulated some assets that could sustain them for some time, they may have preferred to drop out of the labor force by taking early retirement. This has important implications for fiscal policy, implications that have been largely ignored or minimized by some of the proponents of Keynesian economics.

When governments intervene with fiscal stimulus packages to promote aggregate demand, they cannot create the jobs that match the skills that many of the workers that had lost their jobs had acquired. If they tend to do so, by pursuing job creation with an industrial policy twist, they "deceive" themselves, as Hayek had argued in some of his writing and as recent attempts have confirmed. The government does not usually have the skills and the information (or should not believe that it has, without suffering from "fatal deceit") to try to match the additional demand that it creates with the unemployment "holes" that have been created in the economy. The obstacles to job reassignment are not just skill-related, but also spatial in nature. The new jobs might be created in places that are geographically distant from where the individuals who had lost their jobs had been working. Therefore, high transaction costs for workers, required for moving from one place to another, often compound the skill mismatch.

This implies that *when recessions are due to the bursting of bubbles* that have become unsustainable, fiscal stimulus packages will be less successful in reducing unemployment than in traditional recessions, especially in the short and medium run. High unemployment will remain a problem for longer periods of time, as the recent experience in several countries has indicated. We should add, as a hypothesis, that the more developed and complex a country's economy has become, the less effective will become the Keynesian fiscal stimulus packages.

In the circumstances described above, situations will develop that may seem strange. These situations have been reported recently in several countries: high unemployment that exists at the same time as there are many vacant jobs available that enterprises are unable to fill because they cannot find the workers with the right training and skills. This aspect has generally been ignored by traditional Keynesian economics, which, implicitly, has assumed that workers are *fungible,* in the sense that they can be used in whatever jobs become available. Keynesian economics tends to recognize workers that are not specialized and differentiated skilled workers.

An article published in the *Washington Post,* on 20 February 2012, reported that in the "Michigan Rustbelt," where many workers had lost their jobs and where the unemployment rate was very high, "the jobs are already [there]. What is missing are the skilled workers to fill them." The article added that "the phenomenon has become more acute with the recent recovery" and added that "a recent report, by Deloitte for the Manufacturing Institute, based on a survey of manufacturing, found that as many as 600 000 jobs are going unfilled..." The same complaints have been reported in some other countries, including Italy. As economies become more advanced and more developed, this problem of skills mismatch becomes more acute. It is thus possible to conclude with the generalization that the more advanced and specialized economies become, the less effective, in terms of employment creation, the traditional fiscal stimulus packages are likely to be.

There is obviously also a demand side to this problem, because some of the individuals who have lost their jobs want similar, and similarly paid, jobs to go back to work to. The more reluctant they are to accept different jobs, the longer the high unemployment will characterize a country. Especially when a fiscal expansion follows the bursting of long "bubbles," it cannot generate the jobs that some of the unemployed want. As mentioned, a likely result is that many workers, especially older ones, will drop out of the labor market. Some will go back to the countries from which they had come. In the US the ratio of employment to population fell from 62.7 percent at the end of 2007 to 58.6 percent at the beginning of 2012. Only part of this fall could be attributed to the higher unemployment rate.

In conclusion, because in modern economies labor has become much more specialized and less fungible than it was in the past, and because recessions due to the bursting of bubbles reduce disproportionately the demand for labor *in some sectors* and especially *for some skills*, while fiscal expansions may create jobs in unrelated sectors – even when it does not lead to the negative psychological reactions mentioned earlier, or to increasing interest rates – a fiscal expansion should not be expected to be too successful in reducing unemployment, especially in the short and even perhaps in the medium run. The Obama administration and the governments of several European countries have witnessed this problem in the past 4 years.

To the extent that the fiscal expansion may generate higher demand for laborers with skills that are not easily available, it may also create some pressures on wages and on prices *in particular sectors*. Therefore, the inflation rate may fall less than might be expected, given the high unemployment and the low growth rates. Under some circumstances, these selected pressures on wages and prices in particular sectors may set in motion some significant price increases, or some inflationary pressures coming from those particular sectors, in spite of the high unemployment rate for the whole economy.

It should be a concern to policymakers, and especially to central bankers, that, for example, the high unemployment rate of 10.8, for the eurozone, reported in February 2012, was accompanied by an inflation rate of 2.6, a rate well above the one considered desirable even in normal times by those who conduct monetary policy (who presumably aim for an inflation rate between zero and 2 percent). In some countries, including Italy and the UK, the inflation rate has been even higher. One must wonder what would happen to the inflation rate (and to interest rates) if, *ceteris paribus*, the unemployment rate were to fall to, say, 5 percent.

The famous Keynesian view, often cited by economists, that in a depression expansionary fiscal policy could be useful even when the government hired some workers to dig holes in the ground while it hired other workers to fill the same holes – a view that implicitly assumes full interchangeability between the groups of workers that perform the different tasks, in addition to the assumption of easy access to credit by the government – should be placed in the museum of old and discarded ideas, where it probably now belongs.

# 10
# The EMU and the USA: What Are the Differences?

From the time when the European Monetary Union was being created, several American economists, including prominently Milton Friedman and especially Martin Feldstein, in several academic and more popular articles, maintained that the EMU was a "structurally flawed project" that did not have much chance of success or survival. In the views of these and some other economists, mainly from the US and the UK, there were intrinsic and fundamental weaknesses in its design. For Friedman the main problem for the EMU was that of having fixed an important price (namely the exchange rates) permanently, between countries that were likely to have different productivity gains over the years. Friedman was a strong believer in flexible exchange rates and in free prices where the market determines the prices. As a consequence he went as far as predicting a life expectancy for the euro of no more than ten years. (See his 1997 article and Martino, 2008.) It is not clear why this problem would not affect economic relations, say, between California and Texas, which also have a fixed exchange rate between them (they both use the dollar) and that may experience different productivity gains over the years.

Feldstein was more prudent than Friedman in his forecast. He did not make the mistake of predicting both the event and the time when it would occur. He did not predict the precise time of the EMU's demise, but he had also no doubts about the problems that it would encounter as a monetary union, and about its eventual demise (see, inter alia, Feldstein, 1997a and 1997b). Other economists, such as Buiter, questioned whether the fiscal arrangements being made, with rules on the levels of the fiscal deficits and of public debts, would be sufficiently strong to resist the excessive differences that would arise among the EMU member countries.

The paper that Feldstein published in *Foreign Affairs* (Feldstein, 1997a), being published in a popular and widely read journal, attracted particular attention. In that paper Feldstein repeated, for a public that went beyond economists and included individuals interested in policy, his prediction that the ambitious European experiment would be a failure and would even accentuate political differences among European countries. His views were endorsed by many American economists and by financial market operators, who became convinced from the beginning that EMU was a project with fundamental defects destined for failure, and who started making bets on the euro's eventual demise, convinced that their bets would pay off. This attitude would cost many of them a lot of money.

In this chapter we revisit and evaluate some of the main arguments presented by Feldstein, and assess their merit, using recent data that have become available. We shall in particular ask the questions about what differences exist between the monetary union (among *independent* countries) that is the European Monetary Union, and the union (among *states* that are parts of a federation) that is the United Stares of America. Are these differences significant enough to justify the prediction of demise for the EMU?

Perhaps the most important reason given by Feldstein for his pessimism was that the European Monetary Union was far from being an "optimal currency area," a concept that had been pioneered by Robert Mundell, a Canadian-born economist who would win the Nobel prize in economics, in an article published in 1961. An optimal currency area is a geographical area composed by many parts that, because of its intrinsic characteristics, can easily share the same currency. Countries such as Brazil, Canada, Germany, India, Switzerland, the United States, and others presumably constitute optimal currency areas. Latin America, on the other hand, does not. The European Monetary Union was made up of areas or countries with very heterogeneous populations, populations that had widely different characteristics among them, and different histories, traditions, regulations, and government roles.

In Feldstein's view, this heterogeneity would prevent the European Monetary Union from becoming a single market and an optimal currency area.

The justification for the European project was seen as essentially political, to prevent future wars, rather than economic, although there was the hope among its creators that a single currency would help develop a single market and that a single market, by widening the friction-free area for economic exchanges and by stimulating the exchanges and the contacts among the populations, would promote economic development with increasing homogeneity. Feldstein stressed that the EMU did not have some of the characteristics that made the US the successful currency area it was assumed to be. As a currency area, the EMU thus had fundamental flaws that, over the years, would create serious difficulties and would likely lead to the failure of its common currency, the euro.

In his article Feldstein identified especially three basic differences between the US, the currency area using the dollar, that presumably worked well, and the European Monetary Union, the currency area using the euro, that was not expected to work well. Because of these differences the euro project was expected to fail. Feldstein's *Foreign Affairs* article has been frequently cited and has been rewritten and republished by him in different journalistic versions since 2008, when the problems over the euro started attracting media attention. It may be useful to review Feldstein's main arguments to assess their significance, using more evidence and some up-to-date information.

The first important difference, between the EMU and the US was assumed to be the *absence* in the EMU, *of a single labor market,* one that would make it easy for workers located in the depressed areas of some countries, or located in areas with high unemployment, because of area- or country-specific recessions, to move to faster-growing areas, with lower unemployment, in other member countries, thus contributing to adjustment. Feldstein assumed that this happened on a significant scale in the US, where workers could easily relocate because of low impediments to their movements.

On the other hand, various barriers existed in Europe to the movement of workers between different countries that were too rigid to allow easy movements like those in the US. The barriers would prevent the large cross-countries movements, and, consequently, impede or make more difficult the needed economic adjustments. Feldstein mentioned differences in languages, in social insurance systems, in cultures, in religions, and even in union membership. Presumably these differences did not exist in the US, or, if they did exist, were much less accentuated and less constraining than in Europe.

Differences in languages can clearly be important for the movement of persons, although in the past they had not prevented millions of European workers from crossing national frontiers in search of better jobs. They also have not stopped, in recent years, millions of immigrants, coming from territories outside the European Union or from outside the United States, from moving or from trying to move into Europe or into the US.

Although clearly the problem exists and should not be dismissed, the *empirical* importance of this first factor must be questioned. Feldstein's argument does not specify how many workers would need to cross frontiers to make an appreciable difference to the adjustment mechanism. Furthermore, some regulatory and other obstacles (such as union membership and licenses to operate in some specific professional activities) exist also between American states for various categories of workers (as for example for those that require certified professional skills) that have been becoming more numerous. Cultural and religious differences also exist and play some role in the United States, as they do, for example, in political elections. However, it is the quantitative difference that is important and that needs to be addressed.

Recent data, released by the US Census and reported by *Bloomberg News* of 12 December 2012, have indicated that in recent years mobility in the US has been low and continues to be very low, even if it seems to have increased a little in 2012. Furthermore, 64.4 percent of *all* people (of all those of age older than one year) who moved within the United States in 2012 moved within the same county, while another 32.3 percent that changed county moved a distance less than 50 miles from where they had been living. Thus, a full 96.7 percent of all the individuals who changed place of residence essentially remained in the same neighborhood. Only 3.3 percent of the total of those who moved (a total that included small children and retired older people) moved beyond 50 miles.

The Census data show also that many of those who moved a longer distance, who were probably retired, elderly people, moved to vacation places such as Florida, Arizona, and Nevada, rather than to places where employment opportunity was higher. For various reasons – including pensions and health benefits, which may be linked to the enterprises in which one has worked, the fact that moving can be expensive, the quality of the schools, the separation from friends and relatives, the membership of some religious or other group – American workers seem to move little and much less today than they might have done in the past.

Information available suggests that, in the most recent years, the differences in mobility between the US and Europe have largely disappeared. Some recent reports from Europe indicate that large increases in migration, from Greece, Spain, Italy, and a few other countries that have been facing economic difficulties, have been taking place, especially toward Germany.

An effect similar to the one that would be made by workers emigrating from areas with higher unemployment rates to areas with lower unemployment rates may be made by immigrating workers coming from outside the European Union, or from outside the United States. These immigrants are likely to go to the areas that are growing faster and where there are more jobs available, while avoiding, or even moving out from, those with high unemployment. In Italy for example most of the immigrants go to the North where there are more jobs, rather than to the South. There have been complaints from employers in Texas that many Mexican workers went back to Mexico when the Great Recession eliminated many construction jobs where they had worked. This kind of migration of course does not have much to do with whether an area is or is not a single market.

A single labor market with high labor mobility, if it existed, should be characterized (during normal times and, after some reasonable time, after a sustained slowdown has taken place in an area) by broadly similar unemployment rates among the regions that are part of an optimal currency area. The unemployed would be expected to move out of areas of high unemployment and move toward other areas where jobs were abundant. However, recent US statistics, made available by the US Labor Department, and published by *Bloomberg News* on 9 November 2012, indicate that this has been hardly the case in the USA in recent years. Some workers, of course, do move, but not in large enough numbers to make a difference. It may be worthwhile to provide some of these recent data on unemployment in large metropolitan areas located in different states of the US for which data are available.

In September 2012, the unemployment rate for the United States (not seasonally adjusted) was 7.6. However, it varied widely across metropolitan areas and across states, being as high as 28.5 percent in El Centro, California, and more than 13 percent in various cities of California, New Jersey, Arizona, and some other states, and below 4 percent in various cities in North Dakota, Utah, Iowa, Nebraska, and Texas. Considering that, by September 2012, the economic crisis had been going on for at least 4 years, giving ample time to the unemployed workers in depressed areas to move to areas with high employment, it is remarkable that a single labor market area, as the United States is assumed to be, would make it possible for such large differences in unemployment rates to continue to exist, *after 4 years*. We can only conclude that, on this score, the EMU and the US are not as much different as Feldstein and others had believed. Neither the EMU nor the US represents the ideal single labor market of optimal currency areas.

In this connection it must be added that there are also significant differences in the behavior of consumer prices across the US metropolitan areas for which statistics are available, just as there are across the EMU countries. For example, in September 2012, consumer prices in Washington DC, San Francisco, and Seattle rose at the annual rate of 2.8 per cent, while they rose at the rate of only 0.7 per cent in Huston, and 1.4 percent in Miami.

The other two differences between the EMU and the US stressed by Feldstein were (a) the existence of a centralized fiscal institution in the USA, but not in the EMU, and (b) the balanced budget, fiscal rules, for American states, that prevent them from having (large) fiscal imbalances. We shall discuss next these two potentially important factors.

A *central fiscal authority*, similar to the US Federal government, is missing in the EMU. The European Union does not have the power to tax, and the budget that it receives from the *national* governments is very small as a share of the GDP of the EU. This shortcoming was considered an important one by Feldstein. While the US *Federal* government has many powers and receives and spends about two-thirds of all the taxes that the US collects, and can borrow without limits from the market and even in its own currency, in the EMU (or in the European Union) the fiscal action is left almost entirely to the governments of the member countries – except, now, for the "quasi-fiscal operations" of the ECB, operations which according to some economists have become very important but which many would prefer not to classify as "fiscal."

In Europe, there is no central fiscal authority that can play a countercyclical role in a given country, or in the whole region, in case of recessions, as the US Federal government can do and did on a large scale, in the United States, in 2008–09, or in previous recessions. The central budget of the European Union is only about 1 percent of the area's GDP and it is used for specific purposes including paying the salary of the EU personnel. The budget is not used to deal with business cycles. Therefore, EMU-wide (or Europe-wide) countercyclical policy (or for that matter Europe-wide redistributive policy) is not possible in Europe or in the EMU. This countercyclical role is left to the actions of the governments of the individual countries, unless coordination in the response to a recession can be promoted and achieved among them.

This also is clearly an important difference between the two monetary unions because, quite apart from active, discretionary fiscal actions from the US government, in the case of a recession in an American state, some automatic transfers to that state from the federal government may increase. (This can come about through recession-sensitive programs, such as unemployment compensation, distribution of food stamps, and some others.) And at the same time some taxes that the citizens of the state pay to the Federal government (especially income and social security taxes) may fall, because of the fall in that state's income. These actions (built-in stabilizers) are likely to reduce the net effect of a slowdown, centered on a particular state, for that state, while increasing the fiscal imbalance at the Federal level. Feldstein estimated that this reduction could amount to a significant share of the original effect of the recession on a state, although the reduction is likely to vary from state to state.

It should be recalled that the original intention of the Stability and Growth Pact among the EMU countries had been to allow the countries that kept their fiscal account in equilibrium to use up to 3 percent of their GDP to stimulate the economy. This 3-percent-of-GDP spending option would have been helpful in a recession. Unfortunately, as we saw earlier, the 3-percent-of-GDP deficit limit, in the Maastricht Stability and Growth Pact, became a target rather than a ceiling for the EMU countries. Thus, the countries lost most of their potential capacity to pursue a countercyclical fiscal policy, while still respecting the Maastricht rules.

In the USA the *current* situation is significantly different from the one that existed in the distant past, before the Great Depression, when there were no stabilization policies, taxes were much lower than today, and most of the programs that would create some built-in stability (such as unemployment compensation) did not exist. Until the Great Depression the total public spending in the United States *general* government was under 10 percent of GDP; and the spending by the *Federal* government was only about 3 percent of GDP (see Tanzi, 2011a). Therefore, the built-in stabilizing effect of the central fiscal authority was almost nonexistent. Still, the American monetary union (the USA) had survived under those conditions for a long time. Furthermore, as mentioned, unlike the American states, a European country that had kept its fiscal accounts in order (i.e. that had kept its fiscal deficit close to zero) could introduce fiscal stimulus programs (up to the 3 percent of GDP limit). This would have been a significant amount.

This potential fiscal expansion has not been allowed for 49 American *states*, because of constitutional restrictions that prohibit them from running fiscal deficits. Unfortunately, because of the lack of a balanced-budget rule and because of the lax application of the Maastricht rules, almost no member of EMU had kept its fiscal accounts in conditions that would have allowed it to promote a countercyclical policy. When the Great Recession came, the countries were unable to react without breaking the rules, without creating serious consequences for their fiscal accounts, and without running into the problem of high spreads. The spreads would probably have remained low if the original Maastricht rules had been respected. There is now increasing talk in Europe about creating a central fiscal authority, one that could assume some of the stabilizing functions, similar to those of the US Federal government, and perhaps also some of the redistributing functions. We shall come back to this issue later.

The third factor mentioned by Feldstein is the requirement already mentioned, by the constitutions of 49 of the 50 American states, that they must balance their annual *operating* budgets. The states pursue a particular version of the so-called "golden rule," which allows them to borrow for a specific infrastructure that has a long life in order to share the costs of such a project with the future generations who will benefit from the existence of the infrastructure. The requirement to balance the operating budgets significantly reduces the states' annual, official fiscal deficits and the public debts, although they can still accumulate some significant public debts because of their non-operating expenses. Also as James Poterba (1995, p. 331) pointed out, "some cosmetic changes are used [by the states] to meet [their] balanced budget requirements."

In Massachusetts, New York, and a few other states in recent years, the state debts have exceeded 20 percent of their gross state products (GSPs). In 2009, the last year for which data are available, state and local governments (municipal and county) combined had a total public debt outstanding of $2.7 trillion, not a small figure. This debt may now be higher, because of the impact of the economic crisis, which reduced significantly some of the taxes collected by local governments, while at least some states went ahead with various expensive infrastructure projects.

The share of the total sub-national debt accounted by the governments of American *states* in 2009 was 39 percent. That accounted by other *local governments* (counties and municipalities) was 61 percent. Thus, part of the debt has been shifted downward while, as we shall see, much has been shifted upward to the Federal government. The state and other local governments have also accumulated enormous future *contingent liabilities* in their pensions and in other programs for non-federal public employees, because of expected falls in the future growth rates of their economies and in their tax revenue, and because of reductions in the rate of return on the accumulated assets of trust funds. These will create major problems for them, in the years to come, and force them to dramatically cut spending, or raise their tax burdens, as has been happening in some of the EMU countries.

It is also likely that (as has happened in countries that at some point have undertaken fiscal adjustment – for example in Canada in the 1990s), when the Federal government is forced to reduce its public spending in the near future, one area that will inevitably be affected will be the Federal transfers to state and local (i.e. sub-state) governments. Figures from the US Census indicate that Federal transfers to state and local governments combined have averaged about 30 percent of *general* government revenue in recent years. Data from the Office of Management and Budget indicate that the Federal transfers to state and to local governments, as percentages of Federal outlays, have increased over the last 20 years, from about 11 percent to around 17 to 18 percent (see Wildasin, 2009). These transfers have been important to sub-national governments but they are not necessarily countercyclical transfers. As Wildasin (p. 19) put it:

> Much of the cost of the terrorist attacks of 9/11 or the floods produced by Hurricane Katrina [were] effectively shifted to the rest of society through a mixture of explicit intergovernmental transfers, regionally-targeted assistance to local businesses and households and the routine operation of income-dependent tax and transfer systems.

Wildasin (*ibid.*) concluded that

> empirical investigation... [has shown] that intergovernmental transfers play some role, but a modest one, in offsetting fluctuations in local government expenditures and own-source revenues.

Some sizable cities in California (such as Stockton) and in other states have recently defaulted on their debts, because of their inability to meet their current financial commitments. Others are expected to default. Lowered economic growth, unfriendly demographic changes, and over-generous treatment in past years of some categories of public workers (firemen, schoolteachers, and others) have created a menacing combination of negative forces. Once again, one can easily see the similarity to developments in some European countries.

The *gross* public debt of the US general government is now estimated to have reached 107.2 percent of GDP. According to current projections, the ratio of public debt to GDP will keep rising in the next several years (see, for example, the IMF's *Fiscal Monitor*, April 2013, Table 4). It should be repeated that this public debt is still being kept lower by the exceptionally low interest rates that continue to prevail in the US. It would be both a miracle and a worry if these favorable borrowing conditions continued in the future, because they would indicate lack of economic growth. Higher economic growth would almost inevitably lead to higher real rates and lower economic growth would contribute to growing fiscal imbalances.

Unlike what some Europeans seem to believe, the US is not a formal *transfer union,* one in which the Federal government transfers large sums from richer states, or especially from states with lower unemployment rates, to poorer states, or to states with higher unemployment rates as some federations do. State and other local governments have to deal with their fiscal problems on their own regardless how poor they are. Poor states tend to remain poor unless more flexible economic conditions, as for example more flexible labor market rules, create better investment opportunities for investments by out-of-state and foreign companies. The states cannot go to the Federal government for assistance.

If California or some other state (or county or municipality) should run into fiscal difficulties, or even move toward default, the Federal government would have no obligation to come to their rescue. However, the recent and enormously expensive rescue of "too-big-to-fail" financial institutions may have created implicit moral hazards that may in the future raise questions whether there are differences between formal arrangements, which imply no bailout, and implicit ones which may point into a different direction.

In any case, for all the above qualifications, a major difference between the EMU and the US is found in the formal fiscal rules mentioned earlier, which require the American states to (almost) balance their fiscal accounts, and in the existence in America of a central or Federal fiscal authority that plays *some* role in reallocating resources across geographical areas. The governments of the US *states* cannot borrow for *operating* budgets (they can borrow for other purposes), cannot create money to cover fiscal gaps, cannot devalue, and cannot be bailed out by the Federal government, or by the Federal Reserve Bank, in case of difficulties. They can get into fiscal difficulties, and counties and municipalities have occasionally got into major fiscal problems, some in recent months. The states also got into major difficulties in years past, in the nineteenth century, before the fiscal rules were changed.

Thus, the US is in more ways than realized similar to the EMU, except for the fiscal rules and the existence of a large Federal government. Whether the EMU should move toward a set of rules similar to those that prevail in the US for the states, and towards the creation of an expanded European fiscal authority, is an open question and one that is not easy to answer. Some movement in that direction has started. It ought to be understood that for the EMU or for the EU to create a central fiscal authority implies also homogenizing (i.e. making European) many national welfare programs, including pensions, the financing of public health programs, some educational programs, and so on. This is a tall order and one unlikely to be realistic now in Europe, with its widely divergent public expenditure levels and welfare systems.

In conclusion, while the *existence* of the dollar for the American monetary union may not be endangered by the actions of the sub-national American governments, or by that of the Federal government, the *value* of the dollar, or the fiscal situation of the United States, as an entity, can still face problems. The fiscal situation in the US is not rosy and in a macro sense it is not necessarily better than that of Europe, or of the EMU, as an entity. The EMU has a lower *aggregate* fiscal deficit and a lower *aggregate* public debt than the US. The US is clearly facing major difficulties of its own at this time and under current policies may face even greater ones in the future.

It is not evident to this writer that the US Federal government has used wisely the discretion that it has had over fiscal policy, so that Europe should copy the way it has operated. To repeat, the US general government has accumulated an enormous public debt and it will be facing major demographic challenges in future years, challenges that are, to some extent, greater than those of the European countries, especially on the public health front. It remains to be seen how it will get out of its current difficulties. In recent years its level of current spending has moved closer to that of the European countries; however, its level of taxation has remained close to what it was in Europe in the 1960s, even though many Americans, and especially those that belong to the Tea Party, consider themselves to be overtaxed.

Before rushing to adopt the American institutions, and especially before creating a *fiscal or transfer union* in Europe, it would be worthwhile to meditate deeply on the potential consequences of such an action. Transfer unions have worked better in countries where different geographical areas have populations that are broadly homogeneous so that a community spirit prevails, as perhaps it does in Australia and in some countries of North Europe. They have worked less well in countries with less homogeneous populations, like Belgium and Spain, and have created some problems in countries such as Germany and Italy, where transfers across regions are much resented by significant shares of the populations. Large fiscal transfers from rich to poor areas of the same country are resented by those who lose in the transfers, and are never considered sufficient by those who benefit from them. Sooner or later, they lead to political and economic difficulties. Given the large differences that continue to exist among the European or the EMU populations, it seems highly unlikely that the *large* transfers that would be required by a fiscal or transfer union would be tolerated, at least for a long time to come.

Perhaps it is important to reiterate that while *some* of the countries of the European Monetary Union are undergoing difficulties, in part for the reasons listed by Feldstein, but mostly because of excessive public spending by their governments, and by so doing may be putting the future of the euro into question, the current fiscal situation of the United States is not exactly florid. Some states (California, Illinois, Michigan, and others) are facing major fiscal difficulties. They will need to cut public spending and/or, as a less desirable alternative, to raise local taxes by significant amounts to avoid fiscal crises. Neither the Federal government, nor the US central bank (the Fed), nor other states are required or expected to come to the rescue of these states, as some European countries are now expecting similar European institutions to come to their help.

Just as it happened in the European countries, the different fiscal situations of the American states are having some impact on their borrowing costs, in spite of the balanced-budget rules that guide the fiscal behavior of these states. For example, on 15 October 2012, the interest rate on 10-year bonds issued by states ranged from a low of 1.83 for North Carolina to a high of 3.38 for Illinois, a difference of 155 basis points – not as high as in Europe but still significant. The differences are much larger among the counties and the municipalities. The higher interest rates among the states were, broadly, paid by states that had higher incomes (California, Illinois, Michigan, New Jersey, and so on) but were less virtuous in their fiscal behavior, while the lower rates were mostly paid by lower-income and more conservative states, states that had kept their fiscal accounts under better controls. So policies matter, perhaps more than income levels.

The cities that have declared default, because of inability to service their high debts, have done so because there was no savior that could help them as some had expected that the EU or the ECB should have done for Greece, Cyprus and some other countries. It is important to reiterate that, in spite of some role by the Federal government, in reallocating indirectly some tax money across states, the United States is definitely not a *transfer union*. There is much less direct or *intentional* transfer carried out by the central government than many European observers assume. Whatever transfer takes place (for example through the local impact of military spending, of NASA spending, through expenditure for research, or for some social programs) is largely accidental and often not the one needed from a macroeconomic or even from a redistributive viewpoint. There are also inefficient expenditures such as "roads to nowhere" financed by the Federal government.

# 11
# Trade Balances within Monetary Unions

No data are available on the internal balance of payments of American states, or regions. If such data existed they would, for sure, show large disequilibria among the American states or regions, with surpluses in some and deficits in others, just as they do in Europe. For example, when the car industry got into trouble, Michigan, where much of car production was located, must have experienced a major deterioration in its trade balance with the rest of the United States. The states that have started to produce energy from new sources such as shale must have experienced, initially, large deficits in their accounts with other states, because of the capital that they must have needed to import in order to develop the local energy sources. In time the balance will shift in favor of these states, when they start exporting energy on a large scale.

It is not clear to this writer why the current account imbalances among countries should be a bigger problem for those within the European Monetary Union than for other areas; or why the European countries with trade surpluses *vis-à-vis* other EMU countries should be required to pursue policies that would reduce their surpluses and their competitiveness *vis-à-vis* the EMU countries that are in deficit, as some economists have been asking Germany to do, rather than for the former to improve their own competitiveness, which had been reduced in recent years by dubious policies that had artificially inflated their local consumption and allocated money to unproductive investments (such as housing).

Some countries in East and Southeast Asia (especially Korea and Thailand) that in 1997–98 got themselves into difficulties similar to those of Greece, Portugal, Spain, and some other European countries, and that for a while had huge current account deficits as percentages of their GDP, were able to get out of these difficulties in short periods of time by reversing the bad policies that had got them into trouble. In many cases the adjustment came from cutting bad investments, more than consumption. As Cecchetti *et al.* (2012, p. 12), have reminded us, "the Korean current account swung from a deficit of 4.4 percent of GDP in 1996 to a surplus of 12.7 percent of GDP in 1998." The current accounts of some of the European countries in difficulties have also been shrinking faster than some had expected, partly because of the economic slowdown and partly because of policy actions. In other countries, where the deficits were the result of the importation of capital for productive investments in order to develop domestic resources, as in Australia, the deficits reversed themselves automatically once exports increased, without affecting consumption.

When, instead of reversing the bad policies that created the economic difficulties, the countries attempt to finance them, problems inevitably follow, as experience has shown with countries that over the years asked the IMF for programs of financial assistance. It may be an illusion on the part of policymakers to believe that time always makes it easier for governments to make difficult policy changes, even though time may be required for the adopted policies to become fully operational and to have their full expected effects. Unfortunately, in some cases the presumed need for time to introduce the policies becomes an excuse for inertia and for procrastination.

A crisis often creates opportunities for reforms that must be exploited because they are unlikely to represent themselves. This is why reforms are often introduced during crises. Thus, crises should not be wasted as opportunities to introduce needed policy changes. The workers in the countries that have deficits in the current accounts of their balance of payments, that are not associated with new productive investments, must inevitably experience some losses in their real income, to reduce the imbalances. Over time, these losses would help reestablish equilibrium in the countries' balance of payments. If the deficits had been generated by the importation of *productive* capital, no reduction in real income would be experienced.

Some policies could be adopted to generate so-called *fiscal devaluations* in the deficit countries a possibility that had already been noted by Keynes as far back as the 1930s. When a few years ago, before the crisis, Germany raised the basic value added tax rate from 16 to 19 percent and reduced the employers' social security contribution from 6.5 to 4.2 percent it was engaging in a fiscal devaluation. Fiscal devaluations might help in particular circumstances, but in many cases they are not likely to make significant differences (see de Mooij and Keen, 2012; and Horta Correia, 2011). A fiscal devaluation is one that does not come about through an explicit adjustment of the exchange rate, or though differential rates of inflation, or from large cuts in unproductive activities, but through a reduction in the taxes that increase the labor costs. Rarely are countries' governments in positions to give up large tax revenue, to reduce labor costs sufficiently, without at the same time making major cuts in public spending or increasing taxes on consumption as Germany did and as Italy tried to do in 2012. Naturally, the larger is the disequilibrium, the larger the fiscal devaluation must be and the longer it might take for it to work its way. Often the countries in difficulties do not have much time. Recent information indicates that the disequilibria in the balance of payments of Greece, Spain, and some other European countries may be correcting themselves at a faster pace than some had expected.

A balance of payments deficit that has not been generated by the importation of productive capital is an indication that the country has been living well beyond its means. In such cases it is not obvious to this writer why other countries should have an obligation to maintain this artificially high standard of living of the country's population, even though the *political* difficulties faced by the government of the country in difficulty (a government that might be different from the one that created the difficulties), in making the needed adjustment, especially in a relatively short period of time, must be recognized. Thus, while there is no obligation for other countries, a government that is considered to be serious in making the needed reforms ought to be given as much help as possible just as the IMF has over the years assisted countries in difficulty that made corrections to their policies. It even assisted the UK in the 1970s.

The Dallas Federal Reserve Bank has recently released data that may be of some relevance to determine the relative balance of payments, or competitiveness positions, of American states. The data (reported by *Bloomberg News*, on 16 October 2012) show the real, trade-weighted value of the dollar by American states. They calculate the inflation-adjusted value of the US dollar against the currencies of countries with which a particular American state trades. The index varies from 86.20 in Hawaii, and 91.90 in Alaska, to 121.88 in New Mexico, and 115.12 in Texas. New Mexico and Texas can buy much more with one dollar than Alaska and Hawaii can. Probably distance from markets has something to do with these results. These data may suggest that it is a mistake to assume that American states do not have balance of payments disequilibria among them; or that they all face similar import or export costs. However, the effects of the disequilibria, if they exist, are dealt with by the states themselves, without Federal government assistance. No one would ask an American state to pursue an expansionary policy in order to help another state that is running a balance of payments deficit, as some have been asking Germany to do.

Some authors have also shown excessive enthusiasm for the power of devaluations on the performance of countries in balance of payments and fiscal difficulties, while pointing out that the membership in EMU has removed a potentially valuable policy tool, namely devaluation, that is available to independent countries' governments. It is clear that overvalued exchange rates may at times make it more difficult for countries to export, while encouraging imports, and may require some domestic adjustments, including, where this is possible, devaluation. Some writers have gone so far as maintaining that, for example, Greece could exit from the euro, devalue, put its fiscal accounts in order, and then reenter the euro zone. (See the comment by Martin Wolf (9 November 2011), and letters by David Cameron (15 November 2011) and, especially, by Julian Le Grand (17 November 2011), all published in the *Financial Times*.) These suggestions strike this writer as being remarkably naive.

There have been few cases over the years where devaluations have had the desired effect. Many of these cases have been within the context of programs with the IMF that set other conditions beside devaluation. In those few cases when devaluations were successful they were so mainly because the authorities of the countries that devalued had managed to keep full control of domestic wages and prices and made many other changes at the same time. Therefore real wages were significantly and permanently reduced by the devaluation and not just temporarily.

The problem is that devaluations *immediately* and *always* lead to increased import costs, especially for essential imports that may be difficult to reduce (petroleum, medicines, and some other essential goods and services) as well as the costs, expressed in the devalued domestic currency, of servicing the country's foreign debt. The effect of devaluation on exports is always more *uncertain* and *delayed*. Thus, at least in the short run, devaluations are not likely to help much, unless they are accompanied by other policies, and during crises it is the short run that is important. Only when a country exports commodities, in a period when the prices of the commodities are high and are defined in dollars, and when it stops servicing its foreign debt, as happened in Argentina in 2002 and later years – only then will its balance of payments situation *perhaps* improve in the short run. In other cases, as happened to Italy before it joined the EMU, devaluations helps keep countries alive but in the emergency rooms, rather than restoring them to full health.

The effect of devaluation depends largely on what happens, after the devaluation, to domestic wages and prices. Wages may be immediately increased, because of pressures by labor unions, because of street demonstrations, or because of monetary policies (if the country controls the actions of the central bank) and fiscal policies that the government adopts after the devaluation. These policies might easily neutralize the direct impact of the devaluation on the balance of payment of the country. Of course, that effect depends also on the reaction of the other countries with which the devaluing country trades.

In conclusion, Feldstein and others may have overemphasized the differences that obviously exist between the EMU, on one side, and the United States, on the other, *as monetary unions*. On closer scrutiny, some of the assumed large differences between the two monetary unions are just not there, or are less important than they have been assumed to be. The most important differences exist in their fiscal constitutions and in the role that the Federal government plays in the US. However, whether the latter role gives an advantage to the US that leads to beneficial policies is an open question, given the current fiscal difficulties faced by the US.

In Europe, (large) fiscal deficits have been experienced by some (though not all) of the *individual* EMU countries. In the US, they are not experienced so much by the individual states. Rather, the fiscal pressures have been pushed upward, to the Federal government, and perhaps downward, to the counties and municipalities, because when the states are in difficulty they reduce the transfers to the counties and municipalities and reduce some spending that is directly important to the latter.

Both the EMU and the US are now in deep fiscal trouble, and both will require large adjustments to their fiscal accounts in future years. In Europe the adjustments must come at the individual-country level and must thus be differentiated among the various countries. In the US they must come both at the sub-national level and especially at the level of the Federal government, which has accumulated the largest debt and is still running very large fiscal deficits. Which adjustment will prove easier to make only time will tell.

In the EMU the immediate danger may be the impact on the euro, its common currency, because of legal arrangements that presumably make it difficult for a country to leave the EMU. Those arrangements may of course not prove to be unchangeable over the long run. In the US, it is the potential impact of delaying the fiscal adjustment that would be needed to reduce the fiscal gap that may present the greater danger. The US Civil War settled the issue of whether a state could leave the federation.

The number of countries that will continue to use the euro might have to change, if some countries that will not be able to make the necessary adjustments are, sooner or later, forced to leave the EMU. This would create major short-run difficulties for countries whose banks have lent much money to the countries that exit. It should be possible to the euro to survive this change. The number of American states that will continue to use the dollar will not change, in spite of occasional threats by the governors of some states to separate from the US (see Texas). But the states may have to live with a weaker dollar. In fact there has been a significant weakening of the dollar vis-à-vis the euro in spite of Europe's recent difficulties.

The belief that the US is a transfer union, and that the kind of institutional arrangement that exists in the US facilitates economic adjustments by allowing large transfers between states during recessions, is likely to remain a belief, alongside a wish for similar arrangements on the part of some Europeans. Such a union, if it existed in Europe, might simply kick the fiscal problem upward, from the single member states to the federal European government, as it has done in the US, and as some commentators would like to see.

Some other arrangements, aimed at making the European Union and especially the European Monetary Union a more effective and deeper single market, could and should continue to be developed. Regulatory differences should be reduced while at the same time some unnecessary regulations are eliminated. The recent decision, in December 2012, to create a single bank regulator, the European Central Bank, for the 200 largest banks in the European Monetary Union, is potentially important because of the role that banks have played in the crisis. Starting in March 2014, the ECB will have the power to supervise the large banks but it will also be able to overrule the national supervisors of smaller banks, when it believes that those regulators are being excessively influenced by local politics, as for example when local small banks buy too much debt issued by national governments. This step toward a single market should prove to be an important building stone in the final architecture of the European Monetary Union.

Also, greater efforts should be made to better harmonize the tax systems of the European countries, which continue to differ more than they should. Various attempts in the past in this direction have not been successful and this is another area in which the US and Europe remain different. With the greater harmonization of tax systems that would inevitably reduce the differences in tax burdens of the different countries, the need to bring more harmonization in the countries' welfare programs would also become more evident. This is where the differences between the US and Europe remain large. In the US the programs of social security (pensions and health expenditure) are uniform across the states, while they are widely different among the European countries. A more unified Europe would have difficulties with these large differences.

# 12

# On Central Banks' Payment Systems within Unions

While Feldstein gave a lot of importance to the labor market, stressing that Europe's was not a single market, and to the role of fiscal rules and of the existence of a central fiscal authority in the US, he ignored, or downplayed, other factors that might also be important. One of these is the specific arrangements that exist, within the US and within the EMU, that make it possible for private banks, located in different states within the US, or in different countries within the EMU, to have financial relations between them and to move funds from one part of the union to another part. These arrangements may be influenced by financial crises, which may reduce the trust that banks have in each other, and affect the normal relations that exist between them in normal times. They may also influence the way crises develop over time.

Within EMU, a private bank, located in a specific country, say Greece, that has to make a payment to a bank or an enterprise in, say, Germany, must obtain liquidity from the central bank of Greece that, in turn, being part of the European Union's central banking system, can obtain reserves from the ECB. In the US a private bank located in a given state, say Virginia, that must make a payment to someone in Texas can send a check that would be deposited in a Texas bank and then processed through the regional branches of the Federal Reserve System in which Virginia and Texas are located. In normal times the private banks, if they need to, can get credit easily from other banks located anywhere in the United States. During crises these interbank loans become much more difficult to obtain. In 2008 the repo market (in which banks obtain funding from other banks by pledging securities) fell sharply in both the USA and in Europe creating a credit crunch that forced the central banks to come to the help of the private banks.

The Federal Reserve System is not a unified institution but is, rather, made up of 12 regional Federal Reserve banks, or districts that cover all the US states. Some of these banks have also branches, of which there are 25. The three largest Federal Reserve Banks, or districts, in terms of assets, are New York, Chicago, and San Francisco (see Mishkin, various editions, or Mayer, 1998, for descriptions).

In some periods it becomes easier and cheaper than in others for private banks to rely on the discount windows of the central banks, in order to get the reserves they need, to be able to make loans to regular customers, or to make other kinds of investments including loans to hedge funds and other borrowers. In recent years, starting in late 2007, it became less hard to do so. In the words of two financial commentators on the Fed, "[b]anks were able to tap the window for loans at rates below the market after subprime mortgage default contributed to record losses and credit markets began to seize up" (see Torres and Ivry, 2011). The discount window of the Fed became "an inexpensive source of funding" for banks in trouble, a kind of "public subsidy." The cost of borrowing from the discount window went down and the terms of the loans were progressively relaxed. Furthermore, the Fed accepted a wider variety of collateral for loans, applying haircuts or discounts depending on the quality. The Dodd–Frank financial law now requires the Fed to publish discount window loans that until the law was passed were subjected to confidentiality in order not to damage the reputation of the borrowers.

In the years before the financial crisis, up to 2007, it had already become easier and cheaper than in earlier, normal times to get the funds needed from the central banks or from other sources to make loans. However, during the Great Recession the sources of financing banks changed owing to many of the private sources, where banks could get credit, drying up because banks feared having other banks as counterparties after the failure of Lehman Brothers Holdings Inc. Trust on which this market had depended became a rarer commodity. At the same time, borrowing from the central banks became easier, because of the monetary policies they adopted to counter the recession. For that purpose, through their monetary policies the central banks reduced dramatically the long-term cost of borrowing, which besides reducing interest rates may have created some perverse incentives that could lead to the creation of new "bubbles" and future problems.

The private banks can use the funds they have available, from whatever sources, to lend for activities in the private sectors (activities which may be associated with good or bad investment decisions, or that support household consumption) in their own countries (if the banks are in Europe), or in their own states or Federal Reserve districts (if in the US). They can also use the available funds to buy government securities (of their own governments or of other governments), or to make loans to banks that are located outside their jurisdictions.

A lot more money than in earlier times crossed national or state borders in the years before the financial crisis, when lending between private banks located in different places was common. Therefore, the current account imbalances that existed within the EMU were easily financed through capital transfers that took place between the private banks of different countries. They generally did not result in accumulation of claims, at the central banks' level, on the part of some national central banks. The money transferred ended up being invested in the places where housing activity was most intense or where the sovereign debt and the fiscal deficits of countries, or of states and of other sub-national governments, were larger. It may also have financed some consumer spending, which had been inflated by the government spending, outside of the area where the private banks, from which the money had originated, were located.

As already mentioned, when the crisis started in 2008 and was followed by the default of some large banks, there was a sharp reduction in loans made among the private banks, because of the reduction in trust that took place, accompanied by growing concerns about the risk of not being repaid for credit granted. To some extent, depending on one's political perspective, the central banks were forced to step in to fill this gap. In the EMU, the private banks of several countries became more dependent than previously on loans from their *national* central banks, which in turn became more dependent on the *European* Central Bank (the ECB). In 2012 the ECB introduced a program of cheap loans to banks that was equivalent to €1 trillion. Since the beginning of the crisis the ECB had been helping the European banks that needed it to get capital more cheaply than in the past, to facilitate lending to both the private sector and also to governments.

In the US the Fed has been doing something similar, expanding the resources in the banking system. On 12 December 2012, the reserve balances of the Federal Reserve Banks included $1144.7 billion that were made up of $928.8 billion of "mortgage-backed securities" guaranteed by Fannie Mae, Freddie Mac, and Ginnie Mae, and $215.9 billions of other Federal Reserve assets that included credit extended by the Federal Reserve Bank of New York to eligible borrowers through the "Term Asset-Backed Securities Loan Facility." There is evidence that some imbalances have accumulated between some of the 12 regional Federal districts.

In the Fed system the settlement of claims among branches is not immediate but it can take place as far as a year after the clearing of the claims has taken place. Normally it took place in the month of April of each year. Until the time when the settlement took place, "[t]he final debt has been transferred upward, in the books of the regional Federal Reserve banks. But [during this time] this final debt has yet to be settled" (Koning, 2012, p. 2).

The financial flows and the intermediation function played by the central banks can contribute to creating large (temporary or permanent) unbalanced claims between the jurisdictions that exist within monetary unions. For example, beginning in 2007, the Deutsche Bundesbank (the German central bank) and the central banks of the Netherlands, Luxembourg, and Finland started accumulating large claims against the rest of the Eurosystem. By 2012 these claims had grown to between €700 billion and €800 billion against the EMU southern countries, which were undergoing financial difficulties. The largest claims were against Italy and Spain, with smaller claims against France, Greece, Ireland, and Portugal. The replacement of loans among private banks with loans from central banks had contributed to the accumulation of the claims by the German Central Bank and by the other central banks.

The imbalances and the associated claims that develop among *national* central banks in Europe are reported in a settlement system referred to as TARGET2. TARGET2 is one of the largest settlement systems in the world. It started its operation in 2002, after a decision by the ECB Council. The imbalances that develop among the US Federal Reserve Banks' districts are reported in the Federal Reserve's Interdistrict Settlement Accounts (ISA). In its original version the

ISA payment system is much older than TARGET2 as it goes back to 1915 after the Federal Reserve System was created.

TARGET2 refers to the real-time "large-value cross-border net payments and settlement system," the system that keeps score of the large transactions, conducted across countries in the EMU, that are channeled by financial operators through the national central banks. It is operated, on a single technical platform, by the Eurosystem, and clears electronically the daily payments that go through the national central banks. It credits the accounts of the creditor countries' central banks and debits the accounts of debtor countries. However, while the accounts are *cleared* daily, in TARGET2 they are not *settled*. The final settling of the accounts is postponed indefinitely and the accounts can accumulate to reach large amounts, as they have in the case of Germany so that by 2012 its central bank had accumulated claims of around €700 billion against other central banks. The central banks of the debtor countries pay an interest that is collected by the ECB and is credited to the central banks of the creditor countries. The accounts are never settled, do not have maturity expiration, and do not require collaterals. Thus they can become permanent loans made to the debtor country by the creditor country.

In the US the Interdistrict Settlement Account (ISA) was created, in its original version, in 1915. At that time it was called the Gold Settlement Account, because the net balances among Fed banks were settled in gold, on a daily basis, with gold balances that were kept by the regional Federal banks at the Federal Reserve. With time the ISA went through several important modifications. First, the accounts were no longer settled on a daily basis and in gold, but on a yearly basis and in securities of the US Federal government. The debt balances were held in the System Open Market Accounts (SOMA). The government securities which were used as collateral were obtained, not by the banks themselves, but by the Federal Open Market Committee, on behalf of the Fed banks.

In recent years the requirement that the accounts must only be held in the securities of the Federal government was relaxed, to accommodate the qualitative changes in monetary policy, such as the use of quantitative easing. With these changes the Fed has been acquiring assets different from and more diversified than those that it used to acquire in past years, such as, recently, mortgage-backed securities. Also, as mentioned earlier, the regular settling of claims has been relaxed. Some accumulations of claims, by the New York Fed against other Fed banks, such as the Richmond and the San Francisco Feds, are now allowed. It is easy to begin to see some parallel developments between the European Monetary Union and the American Monetary Union in this important area. However the two systems still remain different, mainly because in the US they are periodically settled while in the EMU they are not.

Until 2007 there had been no accumulation of significant financial claims among the specific central banks of the member countries of the European Monetary Union, or accumulation of claims against other members' central banks. The claims, in all directions, had tended to balance one another. The recent, large accumulation of claims by the German central bank, the Bundesbank, and some other EMU countries' central banks, since the crisis began in 2008, has led to questions of why this has happened. What factors caused the large accumulation and what activities had the €800 billion or so claims financed? Was this an indirect or backdoor way to finance continued excessive spending by some of the crisis countries?

In 2011–12 the above questions led to a heated debate in Europe. The debate was initiated by some writing by a German economist, a professor at the University of Munich, Hans-Werner Sinn. He brought to the attention of the public the accumulation by the Bundesbank of claims against other central banks. He has also raised questions about the differences that may exist between the relevant institutional arrangements in the European Monetary Union and in the American Federal Reserve System, which were discussed above. Sinn called for a change in the European system to make it more similar to the American. We will briefly discuss these complex questions that continue to attract heated debate, after a brief digression.

Several economists believe that, after the gold standard system came to an end, and after the Bretton Woods system of fixed exchange rates (which had replaced the gold standard) also collapsed, in the early 1970s, the two earlier systems, which had placed some limits on the financing of fiscal deficits, had been replaced by one that made it easier to run large deficits. Before the change, the deficits had to be financed mainly from a country's domestic sources, which were often limited. After the collapse of the Bretton Woods system and after the liberalization of capital movements and the globalization of financial markets, it became easier for countries to run large balance of payments deficits and for governments to finance larger fiscal deficits. Governments and private agents no longer needed to finance their spending from domestic sources or settle their debts in currency backed by gold. They could settle their debts in paper money, as long as the creditors were willing to accept that money. Current account deficits and fiscal deficits could be financed by capital inflows, as long as there were creditors willing to lend money either in the currency of the borrowing country or in other currency, often the dollar. Over the past decade China has been so willing. This change gave some advantage to countries that had money used as reserve currencies, such as the dollar, and, until 2008, increasingly the euro. These were seen as highly liquid and safe currencies.

Capital flows may be potentially as important as the flow of workers, to help equalize the economic developments of different geographical areas, especially within monetary unions, or even within countries that are not part of a union. The capital that is borrowed can be used to finance public spending and, when the need arises, to try to contrast the economic effects of economic downturns. A country negatively affected by a recession or a slowdown can borrow from other countries, thus reducing the potentially negative impact that its government's borrowing could have on the private borrowing within the country. Instead of reducing their private and public spending (i.e., instead of *adjusting*), countries facing economic difficulties could try to maintain their economic activity by *financing* the imbalances from foreign sources.

However, there is often a limit to borrowing. When the financing opportunities are no longer available, at least at reasonable cost, an independent country would be forced to make economic adjustments on its own, or go to the IMF for *temporary* financial assistance through a Fund-supported program. The IMF and the country would negotiate a financial program and the IMF would provide the needed financing, but with "conditions" attached. The conditions would require the country to *adjust*, normally by restricting credit expansion, by reducing its fiscal deficit, and in some cases by devaluing its exchange rate. The financing that the country had obtained would give it more time, under the monitoring of the IMF, to adjust in an orderly fashion, without putting excessive strain on its citizens.

Until the financial crisis, the belief had been that a country that was a member of the European Union and especially of the European Monetary Union would not need to go, and would not go, to the IMF for a program, because it would be supported by other countries within the Union. Furthermore in such a country the conditions that the IMF might impose could not include devaluation of the exchange rate and a reduction in credit expansion because a member of the EMU no longer controlled the exchange rate and monetary policy. Thus the conditions would be focused on the fiscal variables and on some structural policies such as privatization, labor market liberalization, and reduction of regulations. Once the crisis arrived, the financial requirements of some countries, and especially Greece, proved to be so large that several of the EMU countries were forced to go to the IMF for assistance that was combined with the actions of the ECB and of the European Union. These three institutions formed what came to be called the troika.

Let us now return to the payment systems and to Sinn's criticism. A current and hotly debated question is whether the easier access to liquidity – available to private banks from the national central banks of the EMU, and, indirectly, from the ECB – that the EMU countries have had has allowed them to postpone or reduce the scope of the economic adjustments needed, after the financial crisis arrived. These countries may have been able to continue financing some of their national spending by increasing their liabilities *vis-à-vis* the ECB system of national central banks, at low cost and with loans that did not have a fixed maturity.

Hans-Werner Sinn at the University of Munich and some other German economists have argued that the increase in the above countries' liabilities, that often ended up as claims against the ECB system but on the books of the German Central Bank (and some others), exposed Germany to large potential future losses. The reasoning is that Germany (together with some other countries) has become the country that, in case of a collapse of the Eurosystem, would be left with the largest euro claims, claims that would no longer have market value because they would be against the European Central Bank, which presumably would cease to function. By reducing the quality of the collateral requirements for refinancing credit, and by lowering the cost of borrowing, as the ECB has been doing, it has in some way facilitated this process. (See *The EEAG Report 2012*, pp. 65–70 and especially table 2.1 for quantitative evidence; also Sinn, 2012; Sinn and Wollmershaeuser, 2011.)

According to the views of Sinn and his co-authors, the easy access to liquidity, which the ECB system made possible, especially after 2007, allowed Greece, Ireland, Portugal, Spain, and more recently even Italy, to run larger balance of payments deficits than they should or would have and that were indirectly and cheaply financed by Germany and some other countries. Thus, the former countries had been indirectly allowed to finance their continuing excess spending, avoiding, or at least delaying, the full adjustment needed. If they had been independent countries they would have found this more difficult to do without devaluation and other painful policies. At the same time Germany and some other countries were compelled by the existing system to accumulate large net positive balances against the Eurosystem.

As is often the case in these debates, there is another possible interpretation of the data, as some economists have pointed out. These economists have maintained that the net positive balances accumulated by the Bundesbank and other central banks reflected not the financing of high imports by the countries in difficulties, imports that were visibly falling, after the crisis started, but rather the stock adjustments that were taking place. These were more connected with capital flight than with lack of adjustment.

Various foreign creditors (including banks in Germany, the Netherlands, and other countries) that over the pre-crisis years had accumulated assets in the countries now in financial difficulty had been trying to divest and take their money out of those countries. The stock adjustment was due either (a) to the fact that the crisis in the countries in difficulty had depressed their economies, and reduced the rate of returns or increased the risks in the investments in which the money had been invested, or (b) to the danger that some countries would get out, or be pushed out, of the euro, thus creating a "redenomination" or "currency" risk, a risk that had been assumed to be absent within the EMU. In the words of Cecchetti *et al.*, of the BIS (December 2012), "TARGET 2 [has operated as] a balance of payments equilibrating mechanism inside the common currency area"(p. 4). The fact that the countries in difficulties were members of a monetary union probably made the financing of their current account deficits more elastic and easier. If they had not been part of a monetary union, they would have been forced to adjust more rapidly than they did, once they had ran out of foreign reserves, or to declare default. However this was only part of the story. The other part was the stock adjustment that had caused capital flight from some countries. Thus, Germany and some other countries had replaced precarious investments (the original investments) with potentially precarious claims.

An important point to appreciate is that the existence of the European Central Bank system not only has possibly facilitated the financing (and has thus retarded some of the harsher adjustment process that would have been necessary in its absence, as Sinn and other economists have maintained), but also has "[redistributed] existing stocks of claims from the private to the public sector" (Cecchetti *et al.*, p. 8). It has allowed some banks and other creditors, from outside the countries in difficulty, to reduce their exposure to those countries, shifting the claims to the public institutions (i.e. to the ECB). To a certain extent this has amounted to a potential socialization of private losses, as had happened in the United States, when the Fed and the Federal government rescued the banks that were "too big to fail" and that had made the bad investments in the housing sector that had led to the sub-prime crisis.

Of course, it must be repeated that, if the foreign capital that had been obtained by the countries over the years had been well and productively invested by those countries, then the debtor countries would have escaped the difficulties, or at least some of them. If either those who borrow or those who lend make major mistakes in the decisions that they make, and if the debtors are later unable to repay in full the debts connected with those investments, the blame can be assigned not to the euro but to the bad investments. The same had happened in the USA with the sub-prime crisis.

Similar problems had appeared in the years 1997–98 during the fiscal crisis of Southeast Asia in Thailand, Korea, Indonesia, and some other countries from that region, countries which were not part of a monetary union. These countries got into difficulties for having borrowed a lot of money (from foreign banks when their exchange rates might have been overvalued and the interest rates at which they could borrow abroad were low), and having invested the money poorly, into what turned out to be unprofitable investments, often also connected (at least in Thailand) with construction and construction-related activities such as shopping centers and similar investments.

This is also how the "debt crisis," which caused the so-called "lost decade," came to Latin America in the early 1980s, i.e. to a region where there was also no common currency, or again to Mexico, in the crisis of 1995–96. There was no equivalent of the euro (or the dollar) in circulation in Latin America even though large quantities of dollar bills were being held by the citizens as protection against high inflation and against likely devaluation of the local currency.

A major problem at the time of the 1982 Mexican crisis, and a problem that may have played some role in the European crisis, was the lack of good statistical information available to market operators on what was happening. We saw in an earlier chapter how the fiscal statistics of the countries in the European Monetary Union were being massaged to make them look better than they were. When Mexico in 1982 realized that it was running out of the foreign exchange that enabled it to keep servicing its foreign debts, it discovered, to the surprise of its policymakers, that as many as 1400 foreign banks (*sic*) had been lending a lot of money to hundreds of (mostly public or quasi-public) Mexican institutions, without any central statistical agency keeping track of the total magnitude of the loans. Lack of good statistical information can generate major policy mistakes and can create major coordinating problems. That statistical information is a valuable *global* public good for market operators and also for policymakers especially in a world in which economic activities and capital markets have become globalized.

The Latin American crisis of the 1980s and the 1997–98 financial crisis in Southeast Asia led to a campaign by the IMF aimed at improving statistical reporting on the part of countries, especially reporting with respect to foreign debt. However, debts between countries belonging to the European Monetary Union were not considered foreign debts, because of the single currency that was supposed to have removed "redenomination" or "currency" risks. In the years before the 2008 crisis, situations similar to those of the other crisis probably developed within the EMU: private banks from several of the EMU countries, or even from outside of them, including from the US and the UK, were lending a lot of money to borrowers from within the EMU (including public borrowers) at rates that did not reflect the full, true risk of excessive borrowing. This excessive lending was in part due to lack of full information, about cross-countries private flows of credit, which could lead to difficulties for national governments. It is surprising that until 2007 the interest rate spreads among the EMU countries, which had been very high before the creation of the EMU, remained very low, in spite of the sharply deteriorating fiscal situations of some of the countries that were reported earlier. The spreads after the 2008 crisis mostly returned to the levels that they had been in the 1990s.

Equally relevant, the blame for investing huge amounts of money within that other monetary union, the US, to build houses and to make other investments in areas where they would lose much of their value after being built, should go to those who made the decisions, on both the lending and the borrowing side, and not on the dollar. The potential losses, in the value of the equity that presumably was being created on the stock of houses built, were in the trillions. The banks, mostly from New York, or the "shadow banking system" that lent trillions of dollars for bad investments, in Florida, Arizona, Nevada and other such places, acted in the same way and made the same mistakes as the German or other banks that invested in Greece, Ireland, Portugal, Spain, or in other areas. For example, the Interdistrict Settlement Account in the Federal Reserve Bank of the Atlanta District, which in 2008 had been balanced, experienced a fluctuation of about $140 billion between 2008 and 2010.

The existence of the euro had little to do with these decisions, except for creating the impression that the currency risk was not there, just as the dollar had little to do with the decisions made by American investors. It was a much-questioned, and much-criticized, discretionary decision, by the US government and by the Fed, to come to the rescue of the banks and of other financial institutions, such as AIG, that were involved in the crisis (but not to the rescue of the individuals who had been encouraged or even pushed to buy the houses). No requirement in the constitution that had created the monetary union that is the United States of America could have anticipated or required this rescue of private banks and of other institutions such as AIG and the government-sponsored agencies that guaranteed a large share of the mortgages. Because this "rescue" came on top of fiscal accounts that were already widely unbalanced, it contributed to the making the fiscal accounts even more unbalanced.

The strange thing is that it is doubtful whether the US government, or the Fed, would have come to the rescue of an American state faced with comparable financial difficulty. The American policymakers have shown no interest in coming to the rescue of municipalities that have recently defaulted on their loans. Thus banks continue to have more political power than the sub-national jurisdictions do. With due differences, TARGET2 balances may have played a role somewhat similar to that of the American bank rescue.

One contributing factor to the crisis in Europe may have been that, in spite of the *no-bailout clause* in the constitution of the EMU, the belief had prevailed among creditors that loans to member governments were risk-free. According to BIS rules, loans by private banks to governments through the purchase of government securities did not require the backing of capital assets, on the part of the banks that made the loans. Thus to some extent the BIS indirectly endorsed, or contributed to, the belief that those loans were risk-free.

The perception that, in spite of the no-bailout clause, a state member of the EMU could not default, was widely held by market participants. Thus, American, British, French, German, and other private banks kept lending a lot of money (through their purchase of government securities), to the European governments, and to European banks, even though some of the governments were running large fiscal deficits, allowing the public debts to grow or, in the case of the banks, allowing them to make bad investments. Furthermore the bonds so acquired by the European banks could be used to get additional credit from the national European Central Banks. The American banks have been doing the same in recent years, by lending a lot of money to the American government (and also to sub-national US governments), thus allowing the total gross public debt to reach worrisome levels.

These actions by the banks may have helped the countries or the sub-national jurisdictions receiving the credit to grow faster and to counteract some of the effects of the economic slowdown, by increasing their aggregate spending. However, in time these actions would make the governments run into difficulties in servicing their debts. In Europe this would expose German and other banks to the risks of sovereign default by other EMU countries, and would thus create strong pressures on the ECB and on some of the European government, and especially on Germany, to help the countries in difficulty in order to prevent them from defaulting on their debts. Excessive spending (both public and private) by some countries would come to be seen by many observers as a danger caused by the euro, rather than what it was, a danger caused by the governments of the countries that had overspent.

American banks are also exposed to the risks of default by the states, or the counties and the municipalities, to which they lent their money. The New York banks that had lent money to private or public activities in Arizona, California, Florida, Illinois, or other places also faced difficulties. However, as mentioned, the Federal government and the Fed came to their rescue, fearing the collapse of the whole financial system. They probably would not have come to the rescue of a state or of a municipality that had got into difficulties.

Whether the rescue of the banks and of other financial institutions, rescue that required hundreds of billions of dollars, and that protected the incomes of many of the managers of the banks that had made the bad loans, and the assets of many of their shareholders, was a good or a bad policy remains a controversial issue within the US. The EMU does not have a European-wide government that could have come to the rescue of banks with the tax money of European taxpayers, as happened in the US; and the constitution of the European Central Bank limits its formal role to maintaining price stability. Therefore, in the EMU many of the risks have remained with the banks, whether private or central. Some of the risks have been borne by the *national* governments and not by a European-wide federal government. The European Central Bank has been under much pressure from many quarters to assume that role, thus becoming a lender of last resort and the assumer of the EMU-wide risks.

Another important difference that is believed to exist, between the EMU and the American monetary union, is that, when in Europe significant *spreads* develop, between, say, the interest rate that the German government pays when it borrows to service its debt and the interest rate that the Italian government pays – spreads that are widely and daily reported in the news – many believe that the same spreads automatically reflect the cost of borrowing by German and Italian, or other countries', private enterprises. This effect is absent in the states of the US. As *EEAG Report* of 2012 put it (p. 59):

> In Europe, the risk premiums on government debt spillover to the borrowing costs of residents in the respective country. In other

> words, firms and households in the periphery countries see their creditworthiness and their ability to borrow closely tied to that of their governments.

This in turn has "generated a lethal credit crunch in those countries...," leading to a "deep recession" (ibid.). If it is correct, this rather strong assumption implies that the German private enterprises end up with significant economic advantages over the enterprises of Italy and of other countries with high spreads. The borrowing cost becomes significantly lower in Germany for German enterprises than, say, in Italy or Spain for Italian or Spanish enterprises.

Many observers, including the authors of the *EEAG Report* believe that this is exactly what is happening and that this is giving Germany great and unfair economic advantages. However, this assumption must be verified, and qualified to some extent, in a world where the financial market has become global and where many important enterprises operate globally. It is difficult to understand why, say, Prada, Bulgari, Ferrero, or other large and successful Italian enterprises, or, say Zara, the Spanish enterprise, which operate globally, must borrow in Italy or Spain and must pay the same interest rate as the Italian or Spanish governments, when these governments are seen to have become risky debtors by those that lend them money, while these enterprises continue to be globally successful. Some small enterprises that can borrow only domestically, and that operate mainly locally, might experience higher interest rates on their borrowing, but these rates would still reflect largely different genuine risks associated with the enterprises, and not with the governments, for those who lend them money. They may reflect the reduction in interbank loans more than the interest rates paid by the governments.

Unless the financial market is totally irrational – as some observers believe – the high rates paid by the governments that find themselves in financial difficulties reflect the risks of lending to those governments and not to the enterprises in those countries. In any case, this has little to do with the euro and a lot to do with genuine risk differentials faced by banks, when they lend to different borrowers.

In the US, the fiscal situation of a state (say California) or of a county (say Montgomery County, next to Washington, DC) is also not likely to affect the borrowing costs of a successful private company that operates within the jurisdiction. Microsoft or Apple is not likely to face the same interest rate as the state of California, or as of the county in which they are located. There has been no noticeable exodus of successful enterprises from California because of the current fiscal difficulties and higher rates paid by that state. Furthermore, rates paid on personal loans in the USA have remained high, as high as 15 percent, in spite of the low rates paid by the US federal government.

# 13
# Strategies to Get Out of the Fiscal Crisis

The Great Recession started, as a financial crisis, in the United States, connected with bad investments in the housing market. Soon it changed into an economic recession, and, finally, morphed into a fiscal crisis in an increasing number of countries. In spite of growing worries, so far it has not affected the cost of borrowing for the American government, a cost that has remained surprisingly low in spite of some recent increases in rates. In Europe the crisis had more varied origins and it created difficulties both for countries and for the euro, raising questions whether the euro, as the common currency in the European Monetary Union, would survive the crisis.

The crisis has not ended, and continues to occupy the economic pages of newspapers, and a lot of the time of European policymakers and bankers. One concern has been that some members of the European Monetary Union might choose, or might be forced, to leave the currency area, because of the fiscal difficulties that they have been encountering, especially in connection with the servicing of their public debts. Whether the euro is able to survive the crisis, the effects of the crisis on the economies and on the European populations will be felt for years to come, because of the impact that the crisis is having on the countries' public accounts, on real investment, and on participation in the labor force.

The fall in investment and in labor force participation has reduced not only current economic output but also the potential and future growth of several economies. As a consequence, future tax revenue must also have fallen, increasing the present value of the "fiscal gaps" for many countries, and making the long-run situation of their public accounts less sustainable than it had been before the crisis. This concern about future fiscal sustainability may, in turn, have made some investors less willing to invest, thus contributing further to the future fall in the countries' growth rates and in their tax revenues.

The heated debate, on what to do about the high unemployment rates and about the large fiscal deficits and growing public debts, continues. It puts economists and policymakers, who would like to maintain, or even increase, the countries' fiscal deficits, "until the economic situation returns to normal," against those who are convinced of the need to begin, soon and concretely, to reduce the deficits, through careful fiscal actions aimed mostly at reducing public spending; or, when possible and inevitable, even at increasing tax revenue.

The first group, which includes economists with stronger Keynesian ideology, worries about the consequences, for the economies and for the employment rates, of withdrawing the fiscal stimulus that high public spending, financed by the high fiscal deficits, has been providing to the economies at a time when those economies are still in a weak state. (See various contributions to this point of view in Corsetti, 2012.) The latter group worry about the negative signals that high and growing public debts send to consumers and investors, and about the effects that high public debts, which keep growing as shares of GDP, could have on *future* economic growth, on interest rates, and even on inflation.

Time consistency arguments about policies, which were advanced in past years by some economists, suggest that there could come a time when the governments of countries that had high public debts and that still had control over their monetary policy might be tempted by what might appear to be the easy way out of the current difficulties provided by the promotion of inflation. Some suggestions, of introducing policies that would raise the *acceptable* rate of inflation, have come from presumably responsible quarters, such as IMF staff papers and, more recently, from the new Japanese government.

Of course, financial market operators, who are very sophisticated and who should be assumed to be rational and thus to have rational expectations, are not likely to be caught by surprise (see Tanzi, 1980). Therefore, at some point in time, they may also begin to anticipate the possibility that inflationary policies may be coming soon, leading to higher inflationary expectations and higher nominal interest rates.

This could be the moment when the current large public debts could lead to more serious outcomes, even in countries such as the US the UK and Japan. Nobody can predict when, or if, such a moment will arrive. The relatively well-behaved movements of prices and interest rates so far should not be interpreted, as some still do, as meaning there is nothing to worry about. Crises that involve high inflation and fast-growing interest rates rarely announce themselves much in advance. Unfortunately, economic theory is not like mathematics, even though it makes much use of it to look scientific and to convey a sense of precision. Economic theory cannot determine, in a definitive and non-debatable way, which of the above positions is closer to the truth. It is easy to find leading economists on both sides of this issue. Therefore, recourse to authority cannot help us choose the right position. However, historical experiences are there to tell us about the consequences of high inflation.

Although the broad facts are generally known, there may be some value in reporting a few essential and updated statistics on recent fiscal developments in the EMU and other important countries. For the 17 countries of the European Monetary Union, the ones that use the euro, the general government deficit rose, on average, from a low of 0.7 percent of GDP in 2007 to a high of 5.9 percent of GDP in 2009 and fell to 4.4 percent of GDP in the third quarter of 2012. Therefore, between 2009 and 2012 there was some progress on this score, partly because of the expiration of fiscal stimulus packages and also because of some changes in public spending and in tax revenue. The share of general government gross public debt into GDP for these countries rose from 66.4 percent in 2007 to 90.0 percent in the third quarter of 2012. For the 27 countries of the European Union, a larger group that includes the United Kingdom, the public deficit increased from 0.9 in 2007 to 6.1 percent in 2010 and fell to 4.5 percent in the third quarter of 2012. The general government public debt rose from 59.0 percent of GDP in 2007 to 85.1 percent of GDP in the third quarter of 2012.

The general government overall deficit for 2012, for the four largest European countries, expressed as shares of each country's GDP, was (as surplus), −0.2 for Germany, and (deficits) 3.0 for Italy, 4.6 for France, and 8.3 for the UK. For the United States and Japan the fiscal deficits were respectively 8.5 and 10.2 percent of GDP. The US fiscal deficit is expected to fall by a significant amount in 2013.

In 2012, the shares of the general government's gross public debts as percentages of the countries' GDPs were: 82, for Germany; 127, for Italy; 90, for France; and 90, for the UK. For the United States and Japan they were respectively 107 and 238. In all these countries, with the exception of Germany, the shares are forecast to continue to increase in the next few years. It should be remembered that official projections, like those above, have a tendency to be on the optimistic side. So some unpleasant surprises might be expected.

Among the four largest European countries, the biggest increase in the share of public debt into GDP in recent years took place in the United Kingdom, where it rose from a relatively low level of 43.7 in 2007 to 90.3 in 2012. That share has been forecast to reach 100.7 by 2016. Both the shrinking of the economies, due to the recession, which set in motion the automatic, countercyclical stabilizers, and which lowered the GDPs, and the governments' policy reactions to the crisis, with their "fiscal stimulus packages," explain why the fiscal accounts deteriorated so much, and so fast. The deteriorations in the fiscal accounts of Japan and the United States were also very large, making this a global trend and raising more concerns than in the past about the potential cross-countries effects of the growing public debts and of the policies that sooner or later will need to deal with public debts of such unprecedented, global dimensions.

Reductions in general government revenues, at least as expressed by their shares in the *recession-reduced* GDPs, played almost no role in the worsening of the fiscal accounts of the four largest European countries. During 2007–12, the shares of general government revenues into GDP stayed broadly unchanged, or even increased, in all four large European countries. However, in Spain and in the United States, the share of public revenue into GDPs went down. For the EU countries, taken as a group, there was no fall in revenue. What changed were the shares of the countries' general government expenditures in their GDPs. These increased by 1.5 percent of GDP in Germany; 3.1 percent in Italy; 4.0 percent in France, 3.3 percent in the UK, 3.5 percent in the US, and a remarkable 8.0 percent in Japan. In the US the increase in the 2007–8 period had (also) been a remarkable 7.5 percent.

In most European countries, before the crisis, the shares of the general government's revenue into GDP had been high. Furthermore, there already had been strong pressures, from citizens and from associations of investors, on the governments of most of these countries, to reduce their tax burdens, which were generally considered too high. As we saw in an earlier chapter, some governments had started to react to these pressures by lowering the tax rates. Given the high tax levels, and the mentioned popular pressure to reduce them, it would seem rational to expect that future policies aimed at bringing the fiscal accounts under more sustainable and better conditions would be mainly directed toward reducing public spending, the side of the budget that has experienced the larger increases in recent years and in which most citizens can find programs that they would like to cut, even though often they are programs that benefit someone else.

Some observers, including Mario Draghi, the president of the European Central Bank, have raised the question of whether the European "welfare systems," the expensive systems that in recent decades contributed to the large increases in public spending in many European countries, can survive the fiscal crisis *in their present form,*. Questions about the long-run sustainability of the welfare systems had of course been raised by economists in past years, well before the public accounts were damaged by the crisis, and before the potential growth of the economies had been reduced. This question must have become more pressing after the Great Recession.

With the passing of time, after they were created, many of the European welfare systems became much more expensive than they had been in their original formulations, because of the increasing generosity and higher delivery costs of the programs and because of the ongoing and increasingly fiscally unfriendly demographic and growth trends that had not been anticipated by the policymakers at the time when the systems were created. They required continually higher levels of public spending, as shares of GDPs. These higher levels were first financed by higher tax revenue – which fell progressively more heavily on dependent workers. The higher taxes affected negatively the economic performance of countries. Unfortunately, in spite of their growing levels, the taxes were not sufficient to cover the cost of the higher public spending. The difference required a lot of borrowing by governments, which made the public debts of most countries go up, at times very rapidly.

Already, almost half a century ago (1967), when the welfare states were much younger and much less expensive, in a *Newsweek* magazine article, Paul Samuelson had warned that a reduction in the countries' growth rates and a change in demographic trends would transform the entitlement programs of the welfare states into Ponzi schemes. He had, of course, not been the only economist who, over the years, had make such a prediction, or observation. The current crisis has accelerated the time when the prediction would become a reality and when the warnings should lead to concrete action. Over the years some economists had argued that the welfare systems were having increasingly significant and negative impacts on the economic performance of countries – see as examples Lindbeck, 1995; Alesina and Perotti, 1997; Schuknecht, 2012.

These concerns about the fiscal weight of the welfare states and of the entitlement programs that make them *welfare states* have become more urgent owing to the fiscal crisis. It is of course not easy for policymakers to decide how to respond to the crisis and to the warnings, because many observers believe that the social protection systems (the welfare systems), and especially the more generous, European ones, are among the most important social achievements of the modern world. They have made Europe a very special region, where personal risks and poverty have decreased and this has been done presumably within market economies that preserved significant though reduced degrees of personal freedom. Because of this, many believe that the welfare systems and the safety nets that accompany them should be protected and preserved at any cost.

These questions and the attitudes that they reflect take us to a discussion of possible strategies that could be followed to exit from the crisis. These strategies are related to the policies that the governments of the countries facing major difficulties could or should adopt, with, in some cases, the possible assistance of other countries or of international institutions. Several "exit strategies" have been proposed by various economists. However, in practice, the realistic ones are more limited. We turn now to a brief discussion of these "strategies."

A first and easiest strategy would be that of *doing nothing,* while waiting for some miracle to happen. The miracle could be that of a significant and spontaneous pickup of the economic growth rates. By raising the levels of GDPs at faster paces, economic growth would automatically increase tax revenue, and possibly reduce debt/GDP ratios. This did happen to some countries in the past but it would be wise not to depend on it because the circumstances are now different and all indications are that growth is likely to remain depressed for years to come.

The current debate, about the choice between "austerity" and "growth," is indirectly related to this strategy. It is a debate that seems to imply that countries that already have major fiscal problems might have the luxury of choosing a growth strategy, which would be based on spending more, for infrastructure and for other, presumably, growth-promoting, programs, such as education and research, while ignoring, at least in the short run, the need to control the fiscal accounts. Of course, many countries have the possibility of making some significant structural reforms, as for example by increasing the flexibility of the labor market or the efficiency of the tax systems, or by reducing bureaucratic costs and "red tape." These reforms might not require additional public spending and might have a positive impact on the growth rates. However, they are often politically or administratively difficult to make, and their effects on growth may be significantly delayed in time, raising the problem of what to do about the fiscal deficits and the growing public debts in the short and the medium term.

Unfortunately, miracles may be as rare in economics as they are on the road to sainthood especially when the road for them is not paved by good reforms. It is hard to believe that faster growth could be promoted, under current conditions, by doing nothing, or even by spending more, while ignoring the impact of higher public spending on fiscal deficits, and potentially on future interest rates, as some economists have been arguing. Although there is no question that the countries facing difficulties should make every effort to remove the many structural obstacles that continue to exist to growth, and that the presumed choice between austerity and growth should stress this aspect, in most countries, and especially in some European countries, it would take an act of true faith to believe that, with no change in fiscal policies, or even with an increase in public spending, growth could automatically increase fast enough to become a possible solution to the current economic and fiscal difficulties of many countries.

The longer it took, before growth rates picked up significantly, the greater would be the cumulative deterioration in the fiscal accounts, and the future economic growth rate needed to compensate for it. The higher the shares of public debts into GDPs become, the more difficult it will be to deal with them in the future. Furthermore, a return to a "normal" economic situation, one that would surely bring higher demands for credit, for private investments, and for private consumption, would likely have an impact on the unusually low, risk-free, real interest rates that now prevail in several countries (unless financial repression kept them artificially down). The interest rates would rise in most countries (both those which are now seen to be risk-free and the others), increasing public spending, and making the servicing of the debt more costly and the reduction of the fiscal deficits more difficult.

The strategy of promoting a fiscal expansion to promote economic growth, recommended by some vocal and convinced Keynesian economists, would be pursued by introducing additional "fiscal stimulus packages," either on an individual country basis or in a coordinated manner among different countries – if such a coordination could be achieved, which seems highly unlikely. The strategy would be based on the hope of shaking up the economies towards higher growth rates, on the assumption that the current obstacle to growth is a lack of aggregate demand. However, if fiscal deficits that have been as high as 10 percent of GDP (in Japan, the UK, the US, and some other countries), and that continue to be close to that level in some, have not done the trick so far, it seems highly improbable that deficits even higher than the current or recent ones would have the hoped-for effects. As we argued earlier, the negative impact on economic activities, coming from increasingly precarious fiscal conditions, on the psychology of investors and consumers, would likely neutralize whatever positive effect on growth might be expected to come from the Keynesian demand push.

Some recent econometric work has concluded that the fiscal stimuli introduced at the beginning of the crisis, mostly in 2009, might have had a short positive effect on economic growth, but that the positive effect quickly vanished and left the countries with worse public accounts and possibly with lower growth rates (see Coenen *et al.*, 2012). Therefore, the effect was similar to that of steroids for athletes: possibly (but not surely) improving short-run performance, while damaging that for the long run. As mentioned earlier, some work has tried to estimate the size of the fiscal multipliers, with conflicting results. Generally, the multipliers reported have been lower than they had been assumed to be in the past. Also, as mentioned earlier, high public debts have been shown in many studies to have a negative impact on growth, especially when they exceed some high limit, an impact that may vary from country to country, and, one should add, when several large countries all have high public debts at the same time.

Another strategy, in part linked to the previous one, would be for central banks and especially for the European Central Bank, within the European Monetary Union, to become *lenders of last resource,* not to banks but to national governments, as some economists have been asking for. The central banks would, presumably, buy without limits and at reasonable low rates, either directly from the governments, or indirectly from the secondary markets, to keep the interest rates down, the government securities necessary to finance the public deficits and the replacement of the public debt that reaches maturity, when the countries are having difficulty in replacing the debt from the financial market at reasonable rates. For most industrial countries, the maturity structures of the public debts are now relatively short, between 4 and 7 years.

Some economists, such as Paul de Grauwe, in several publications, have argued that this action (i.e. the financing by the central banks of fiscal deficits) would prevent the yield on public securities from increasing and, more significantly, would not create "moral hazard," nor contribute to inflation. However, this strategy would be close to one that gave governments "ATM cards" to be used to finance their fiscal deficits while the bills for the public spending would be sent to the central banks.

At the moment, most central banks are prohibited from buying public bonds directly from the governments. However, central banks are allowed to buy, presumably in the pursuit of their monetary policy objectives, government bonds from the secondary markets thus creating space for governments to issue more bonds. Pushing the banks to do more with their purchase of public bonds from the financial market would be a risky and dangerous departure. It would effectively change the nature of central banks' operations, from monetary policy into fiscal policy. The action of the central banks would complement that of the tax administrations. Some of the central banks, including the European Central Bank, have already engaged on a large scale in this kind of fiscal policy, and have planned to engage even more in it. One can only hope that the results will be the ones hoped for.

The "inflationary finance" strategy, or the bond-buying policy by central banks, when it was widely used in the past, in Latin American and in other countries, always led to one result, but at times with some significant lags: high inflation – and, occasionally, if the monetary expansion was sustained, hyperinflation. For this reason, until the current crisis came, economists had been almost unanimous in promoting what had appeared to be a successful campaign to make central banks politically independent from governments. The independence of the central banks reduced the danger that they would be used as ATM cards to finance directly the operations of governments. Economists thought that they had won this campaign for central bank independence, until the crisis came. Recent attitudes and discussions among economists and politicians indicate that the victory may have been short-lived, and that memories tend to be short.

In a monetary union, as is the EMU, or the United States of America, or Brazil, this strategy would lead to additional difficulties, besides the likely one of leading to high inflation. Just imagine if Greece in the EMU, or the state of California in the United States, or the state of São Paulo in Brazil were able to finance their public spending by selling their public bonds directly to the ECB, the Federal Reserve Bank, or to the Brazilian Central Bank. This would create the classic problem of the friends that go to a restaurant, where, on the menu, there are expensive lobster or caviar dishes and cheap chicken or spaghetti dishes. If the friends were going to share, collectively and equally, the cost of the final bill, each guest would be tempted to choose the most expensive dishes. Clearly there would be a need to impose limits to each person's spending. But this is what the so-called troika (IMF, ECB, and EU) has been trying to do, with limited but positive success, in some of the EMU countries in difficulty. For this reason, monetary unions do not allow access to the financing by central banks, especially by parts of the union. In Brazil in the past this policy led to disastrous consequences.

Another strategy would be that of convincing the countries that belong to the European Monetary Union, and that have strong fiscal accounts and good credit ratings (a fast-shrinking club), to share in the risk faced by the creditors, or to use their reputation as debtors, to obtain credit on behalf of the countries of the Union that have less good reputations. This sharing of risk could come about in either of two ways. One is through the sale of so-called Eurobonds, bonds that would finance particular countries but that somehow would be endorsed collectively by groups of countries – for example by all the

EMU countries, or by the European Union, if the latter were given a large enough budget. The other is by having a country with a strong reputation, say Germany, to borrow from the financial market and then on-lend the borrowed money to the country or countries in need, say Greece or Spain. For example, on 16 November 2012, Germany could have borrowed money, for ten years, at 1.33 rate and could have lent the money to Spain, which was paying about 7 percent to borrow money with the same maturity, or to Greece, that was paying a much higher rate. The lending to Spain or Greece by Germany could have been done at a rate above 1.33, to compensate Germany for some of the risk that it was assuming. This would probably be the most efficient way to lower the cost of borrowing for the EMU as a whole.

The objections to this strategy are obvious. The first has to do with the German government's willingness, or constitutional freedom, to engage in such a scheme. The second is the impact that additional borrowing by Germany, borrowing that would inevitably increase Germany's (gross) debt, would have on Germany's borrowing costs. The greater were the risk that Germany assumed, related to the risk that it would not be repaid by, say, Greece or Spain, the greater could be the increase in Germany's own borrowing costs. Unless one assumed that the operators in the financial market are irrational, one must also assume that the borrowing costs for Spain or Greece reflect the risk that the creditors, that now tend to be well informed, attribute to their lending to Spain or Greece. Those risks would be transferred to Germany, a country that does not have budgetary surpluses to lend and that has already a sizeable public debt of its own, 82 percent of GDP in 2012.

When the operators in the financial market come to believe that Spain and Italy (or Cyprus, Greece, Ireland, or Portugal) have started their journey, on a safe and transparent road, without surprises, that leads to an exit from the fiscal crisis, the rates at which they lend to these countries will inevitably fall. They had already fallen somewhat for some of these countries in 2012. The rates have been high not because of market irrationality, or because of "speculation," as some politicians or even some economists want to believe, but because the market operators are well informed and rational and are aware of the dangers that continue to exist when they lend money to countries with high debts and deficits, and where governments have to deal with street demonstrations that often influence the behavior of the policymakers that must enact the policies for reducing public spending, or where the policymakers still believe that spending reduction is not necessary and significant structural reforms are not required.

Another strategy, already alluded to earlier, also advocated by a few well-known and influential economic commentators, is that of pushing especially Germany into adopting, domestically, expansionary policies that would aim at reducing the competitive advantage that it acquired over the years (because of the policies that it had followed) *vis-à-vis* some of the other countries of the European Monetary Union. This difference in competitive advantage led to large balance of payment imbalances among the EMU countries. In the views of these commentators, Germany's competitive advantage could be corrected by becoming less competitive, *vis-à-vis* the other countries.

Apart from the fact that it is unlikely that Germany would ever agree to follow such a strange policy, it is not clear what specific policies – besides those in the fiscal area that it still controls, and at what parametric level of intensity –would need to be followed by the German authorities, to achieve the desired economic expansion and the needed inflation that would shrink its current surplus. It must be recalled that Germany does not control the exchange rate or the monetary policy. Furthermore, it already has a high public debt as share of GDP (well beyond the Maastricht limit), and a level of public spending that is also high (around 45 percent of GDP). It has been running fiscal deficits in recent years, though not high ones. If it followed the advice of these commentators, it would not be long before Germany would face some of the same difficulties as its southern neighbors.

As reported earlier it was not a long time ago that Germany was facing significant fiscal difficulties and when some considered it a kind of "sick man of Europe." Twenty years ago Hans-Peter Fröhlich, a German economist could write (1989, p. 21) that "foreign observers are often most puzzled by Germany's poor growth performance... and domestic policymakers' apparent reluctance to change policies..." Furthermore, Germany's trading world is not limited to the EMU countries and especially to the countries in difficulties, whose economies are a miniscule share of the world economy. It operates in the much larger world market. Reducing its competitive advantage, *vis-à-vis* the poorly performing EMU countries, by enough to make a difference to the latter, would reduce Germany's competitive advantage *vis-à-vis* the rest of the would. This would seem to be a high price to pay for a country to accommodate the needs of neighbors that have not always behaved, economically speaking, as responsibly as they should have.

This "pass-the-buck" strategy, including the one that required Germany to become a kind of locomotive for other countries' economies, is not entirely new. It was advocated, in a different context, a quarter of a century ago by some economists, including the late German economist, Rudiger Dornbusch, then a prominent professor at MIT. At that time, the goal of these economists was to promote a kind of *global* Keynesian policy, in the belief that there was need for a *global* aggregate demand of a given level to push the world economies to a good performance. These economists believed that, by pushing countries that had surpluses in their balance of payments to expand, to compensate for deficient demand coming from countries in deficit, world prosperity and full employment at the global level would be promoted.

In a contribution, on policy coordination among countries – to a book edited by Mario Monti, the Italian prime minister in 2012 – a contribution that was discussed by Professor Dornbusch and by two other economists, at a conference organized by Monti in Milan, the author of the present study wrote that the push on surplus countries to expand when other countries were running current accounts deficits reminded him of a fable by Aesop, about an imprudent fox that had lost its tail in a trap. The fox without the tail, felt rather indecent going around without it, so it started a campaign among its fellow foxes to convince them that not having a tail was a clear advantage for the fox community. Naturally the other foxes did not buy this argument and refused to follow the advice (see Tanzi, 1989; Dornbush in Monti, 1989).

We finally come to the strategy that, to the author of this chapter, seems both necessary and realistic, even though it is obviously a politically difficult one for governments to implement. Some of these governments would rather "pass the buck" if they could, than follow the strategy. It is the strategy that realizes and admits that the present level of public spending in many countries has reached a level that makes it increasingly more difficult to finance, and that it will become even more difficult to maintain and finance in future years. In the years to come, it will become harder for many countries to raise taxes by enough to make a difference, or to continue to borrow enough, at reasonable rates, to fill the gap without serious consequences. This is not a cyclical consideration but one that has to do with the medium and the long run. It will thus be necessary for these countries to reengineer the role that the state has been playing in their economy, in order to reduce significantly the level of public spending *over the medium run and longer run*. However, it will be necessary to start *soon* with this re-engineering, even at the cost of some short-run, negative impact on the economy and on employment, coming from expenditure reductions. This negative impact can become an excuse for some governments not to take action soon and an argument for some commentators and economists to recommend the postponement of the adjustment, as they are doing now in some countries with high fiscal deficits and public debts. There is some reason to believe that this message might be finally beginning to be received by some European countries and by some governments, as for example it was received by the Monti government in Italy and by the British government, even though far more persistence will be needed and the populations may not react well to these policies.

It should be recalled that in recent decades and especially after World War Two the economic role of the state, and the public spending necessary to support that role, expanded dramatically, especially, but not only, in the European countries. In all the European countries that are now facing fiscal problems, the share of public spending into GDP shot up in the past decades (see Tanzi, 2011a). It reached levels that would be difficult for many of these countries to maintain, without doing considerable damage to the performance of their economies and without creating problems for other countries. The goal for governments should be to try to set the clock backward, but to do it intelligently, while doing whatever is possible to continue promoting some of the important government objectives, in terms of social protection, as in the past. The government is not the enemy as some have argued, but too much government can have the same bad effect as taking an excessive dose of a needed medicine with powerful side effects.

The aim for governments should be to play their essential role more efficiently and in a far more focused manner than some countries have done. The idea that governmental action can and should deal with all the dangers of modern societies is naive. Governments should focus on preventing hell on earth. When possible, different policy instruments, to reduce or replace public spending and to lower tax rates, should be used. In most countries there are so many inefficiencies and unnecessary or questionable public expenditures, some tied to what could be called the architecture of the public sector, that with fundamental reforms, that addressed the questions of why certain things are being done in a certain way, major expenditure savings could be achieved. Some public employees would inevitably lose their jobs in this slimming-down process but it should be kept in mind that the justification for having a government is to provide public services, and not to create jobs. (For Italian examples, see Tanzi, 2011c).

The full reduction in public spending, obviously to be achieved *over the medium and long run* and not immediately, should be large enough to wipe out the fiscal deficits and to initiate a trend toward the reduction of public debts, to bring them to levels that could become less damaging and easily sustainable. A faster rate of growth of the economy, achieved through essential structural reforms, would help reach this objective. Well-focused "spending reviews" could be tools to achieve this objective. However, such reviews must be ambitious and must include the possibility of restructuring the architecture of the public sector, which often tolerates large public spending that could be reduced or eliminated by changes in that architecture. As mentioned, the reduction in public spending would require, and should be accompanied by, major structural, market-friendly reforms, aimed at making the economies more flexible, more efficient, and more equitable. However, equity, while important, cannot take precedence over efficiency. The policies would help promote economic growth, and would reduce the cost of the transition to smaller governments. The process should make sure that the costs of the transition to a smaller government role are equitably distributed. Both the objective and the perception that the reforms are fair is essential. In most countries there are many structural obstacles to growth that intelligent reforms can eliminate without the need to increase public spending.

Some may judge this strategy a "pipedream." It is obviously not easy, especially politically, because it would be opposed by powerful lobbies that represent the vested interests of those who have been benefiting from the public spending. However, there are examples of several countries – some reported in my recent book *Government Versus Markets* (2011a) – that succeeded, within relatively few years, in drastically reducing the share of public spending and of public debt into GDP. (See also various papers by Alesina and Ardagna, and by Schuknecht and Tanzi, listed in the references.) In some of these countries the reductions in spending exceeded 10 or even 15 percent of GDP within a few years.

These countries (Canada, Finland, the Netherlands, Sweden, and more recently Latvia and Estonia) were able to correct large fiscal imbalances and to reestablish higher rates of growth in relatively short periods of time, while significantly cutting public spending as a share of GDP. There are many papers that have described Canada's remarkable turnaround, from a country with a large spread and with a public debt that had become very high and growing, to a country that for many recent years has had the best fiscal accounts among the G7 countries and frequent budgetary surpluses, while continuing to grow at very good rates. It is also remarkable to point out that, today, Sweden's public spending is lower than that of Italy, while about two decades ago Swedish public spending had reached a level that was as much as 20 percent of GDP higher than Italy's (see Tanzi, 2011a).

Both Canada and Sweden are still considered welfare states even though in both there have been the expected complaints about the cuts in social spending. In Canada the complaints have come from sub-national governments and from people with leftist biases (see, for example, Courchene, 2006). For a broader but mostly statistical picture of examples of fiscal consolidation in the world, see the IMF paper by Ali Abbas and others (2010, especially table 3.2 on p. 16).

In a recent interview with the *Financial Times* (16/17March 2013, Life and Arts section, p. 2), Fredrik Reinfeldt, the prime minister of Sweden, provided an illuminating comment of how Sweden succeeded in getting out of the dramatic crisis of the yearly 1990s when it had several years of negative economic growth and horrible fiscal accounts. He mentioned that in the late 1980s Sweden was "the world's record-holder in high taxes...with a tax burden of about 51 percent of GDP." In the 1990s, "Sweden was forced to impose painful cuts" in public spending and the tax burden was eventually reduced to 44 percent of GDP. Tax rates were reduced and several taxes were abolished. The result was that the country recovered and now it has the public finances in balance and the public debt has been lowered to 40 percent of GDP. It took 20 years of tough reforms but now "the country [is] is known for its strong economy and its competitiveness."

The Prime Minister summarized his view of the main things to do. Namely: (1) do not cover bank losses; (2) do not subsidize companies in trouble; and (3) cut benefits. His concluding remark was also very important: "[ when major reforms are made] fairness is vital to get popular support." Unfortunately fairness has been missing from many recent adjustment programs in the EMU countries. Perhaps it should also be repeated that there is always a time lag between the time when the reforms are made and the time when they generate the desired results. Because of this dangerous time lag, the initial effects of the reform, that inevitably bring some pains, will often turn the population against them and induce governments that may still believe in miracles to abandon them before they have their effects; or what is the same convince some that they may soon be abandoned.

In an op-ed in Bloomberg (7 January 2013, "Why Austerity Works and Stimulus Doesn't") Anders Aslund summarized the recent experience of Latvia which is also illuminating. The financial crisis hit Latvia dramatically, leading to a fall of 24 percent in GDP. "In 2009 Latvia carried out an arduous fiscal adjustment of 9.5 percent of GDP"... "Yet [in 2011] Latvia's economy grew by 5.5 percent, and in 2012 it probably [grew] by [another] 5.3 percent... " Aslund added that in a crisis, "taxpayers think the government should tighten its belt when they are forced to do so" and that "it is much easier to cut public expenditure than to raise revenue."

Still another interesting experience with fiscal consolidation during the recent crisis is that of Estonia. In an article "Fiscal Consolidation in Estonia," the deputy secretary-general of fiscal policy of Estonia, Ivar Sikk, reported (in OECD's *Great Insight*, volume 1, issue 3, May 2012, p. 18) that "[w]hen trade collapsed in late 2008, Estonia's exports plunged by nearly 50% during the first half of 2009 and financial flows in the banking sector almost stopped." ... "Immediate measures were taken to maintain the credibility of state finances and to keep fiscal position within Maastricht limits." "No budget lines were saved from consolidation" and most public programs were sharply cut. There were also some revenue increases. "The Estonian economy emerged from the crisis with a substantially stronger fiscal position." The fiscal consolidation during the 2008–10 amounted to

17 percent of GDP. As with Latvia and earlier with Sweden, "[n]o budget lines were saved from consolidation." "The consolidation need was well taken on board by the society – there were no protests in the streets . . . "

What may appear surprising about these experiences is that the countries that made the large reductions in public spending, reductions that were large but fairly distributed and combined with important structural reforms, returned relatively quickly to growth, and managed to retain the highest ratings in international indices of social welfare. They continued to provide to their citizens high levels of socio-economic indicators, and to score high in human development indices, estimated by the United Nations and also in other indices. In other words, the important social objectives of these countries, and their growth rates, were not compromised by the spending cuts (even though before the cuts were made the economies had at times experienced major output reductions) and by the structural reforms that accompanied the cuts. The view that social objectives are always damaged by expenditure reductions is simply not correct and does not recognize the fat that often accumulates in government programs over the long run.

In the next chapter we return to the more general question of the reduction in public spending, to argue that it may not be necessary to destroy the welfare state in order to bring to the countries the necessary reduction in public spending. However, it is often necessary to return as far as possible to the original goals of the welfare states, ridding the programs of the free riders and of the inefficiencies that have grown over the years and that have contributed enormously to making them more expensive than they had initially been intended to be.

# 14
# Is There a Fundamental Law of Public Expenditure Growth?

There is an important aspect of the growth of public spending that has not attracted the attention that it deserves and that may be an important element of an exit strategy based on reducing public spending over the medium and long run. It is an aspect connected with what could be characterized as a *"fundamental law of public expenditure growth over long periods of time."* It is a *law,* or at least a consistent *trend,* that has attracted little formal attention, even though it seems to have contributed much to the long-run growth of public spending in many countries, after the original welfare state programs were created in distant decades. The law focuses on the growth that took place in the public spending of many countries in the years *after* the introduction of the landmark social legislations, in Germany with Bismarck, in the US with Roosevelt and Johnson, in the UK with Beveridge, and in other countries with similar legislations. (See Tanzi, 2011a: ch. 5.) The law focuses on the fact that public spending growth often comes in small steps and not in big jumps.

This *fundamental law* bears some similarity to the famous *Wagner's law* but is distinct from that law in its motivation. It is more connected with the literature on *public choice* than with the *normative theory,* which assumes that market failures require explicit public intervention by governments and, often, more public spending. As a consequence the additional spending is both desirable and justified. Unlike Wagner's law, *the fundamental law* makes the growth of much public spending almost an accident and a potentially costly but avoidable one.

An important question is whether the effects of the *law* can only work in one direction. As mentioned in the previous chapter, the experience of some countries indicates that, given the needed political determination, the effects of the law can be stopped, or they can even be reversed, thus making possible for the governments of countries the reduction in their public spending.

The *law* states that most government programs, which are created at some point in time, and which when they are created require some increase in the level of public spending (as a share of GDP), have a tendency to grow, almost continuously and spontaneously, over future years and to become more expensive unless close surveillance and close monitoring, to keep the costs down, is placed on them. The growth in spending is also not due to *Baumol's law,* which argues that the productivity of the public sector's activities tends to grow less rapidly than that in the rest of the economy (see Baumol, 1967) thus making public spending grow as a share of GDP. The statistics of most advanced countries indicate that a large part of the growth in public spending in recent decades in those countries has come from transfer payments, often made in cash, rather than from the *real* or *exhaustive* expenditure of the governments, which is the part more exposed to the effects of Baumol's law. The real public expenditures have grown much less than the public transfers (see Tanzi, 2011a, p. 10, table 1.2). Like many people in today's rich societies, public programs start slim and, often, focused on limited deserving groups, but tend to acquire fat as they grow older. It takes strong determination on the part of governments, as it requires on the part of people, to stop, or reverse, that tendency.

There are several contributors to this trend. We will discuss them briefly. A fuller and more exhaustive description will have to wait for another occasion.

The **first** is that the public programs, that may have been intended by the initial legislation to assist *small* and *well-defined* groups of deserving beneficiaries, with the passing of time attract additional *users* to them. These additional users can be considered, in some sense, as *less deserving,* or even *free riders.* These additions create horizontal inequities in the programs, between the initial and clearly deserving beneficiaries and the later and less deserving ones. Of course programs that are truly universal from the beginning and at a given real level of services or benefits that cannot change would not enter in this category, because all the citizens would qualify for them from the time when the programs are enacted.

The **second** contributor to the law is that, in addition to attracting new users, whether the government programs started as being limited to particular groups or as universal in their coverage of beneficiaries, they tend to attract additional *providers,* because of the expansion of the number and of the quality, or scope, of the services that the programs provide to the users. Therefore more public employees are needed to deal with the expanded programs and services. This expansion may be seen as natural. At times it may be connected with technological progress (as in the health sector) or with changing sociological views (as in the educational sector). For example, should a *basic* public health service justify the provision of very expensive drugs (some costing hundreds of thousands of dollars per year) that come into the market and that may simply prolong the life of a person that is already ill by a few months as some of these drugs do? The government would, of course, not have the option of restricting the use of new technologies and the *production* of new expensive drugs that may contribute little to the welfare of the citizens. However, it could restrict its *financing* of the use of new products or services that cost a lot but bring marginal benefits. It should be realized that as new drugs continuously come onto the market government costs go inevitably up without any change in legislation.

The **third** contributor is that, with the passing of time, most public programs develop various forms of what economists call *technical* inefficiencies or what could be called bureaucratic cholesterol. They become progressively less efficient than they need to be in delivering the services for which they are responsible. Without the inefficiency, the services could continue to be provided more economically.

There may be a **fourth** contributor. As the number of objectives that the government wants to achieve with its spending programs changes and becomes more complex, more public personnel are needed to monitor whether the objectives are being promoted. It is not clear whether this development should be linked with inefficiency, and be considered a part of it, or whether it is a distinct and separate one. However, in either case, the result is to lead to more costly programs.

We will discuss in turn these categories of contributors to the growth in public spending, and provide some real life-examples, from different countries. It should be evident that the examples are chosen at random. Other examples from different countries could have been chosen.

Let us start with *the expansion of the number of those who benefit* from the government programs. The *less deserving,* or the *free riders,* individuals that, through public pressure or other means, succeed in getting access to the public programs, *after* the programs have been created, are individuals who had not been included, and had not been intended to be included, in the spending programs, when these programs were first created. The original spending programs had been intended to assist well-defined and limited groups of beneficiaries that seemed to truly need the governmental assistance. However, with the passing of time, and often through political pressures and administrative maneuvers, through lobbying of politicians, or even through poor governance, or acts of corruption on the part of public employees, growing numbers of *free riders* manage to be included in the programs. This may happen years after the original programs had been legislated. This swelling of the numbers of beneficiaries tends to be a cumulative process over the years unless a stop is put to it. The *free riders* become part of the groups of citizens that are entitled to benefit from the public programs, thus expanding the original group and making the programs progressively more expensive than originally intended.

The greater are the benefits of the programs to individuals, the greater will be the lobbying efforts by the potential beneficiaries which had not been originally covered, and the pressures to extend the coverage. The additional users will present arguments, and some evidence, that they deserve to be included among the programs' benefits. Through their lobbies they will pressure the politicians and the public administrators to support their claims. Because the addition of new beneficiaries will be gradual, and at any one time it is likely to be small, they will not elicit as much resistance as does the public spending associated with new programs.

This internal growth has characterized many government programs in various countries: those for disability pensions; those for qualification to receive public pensions, because of some relationship to individuals who had paid the social security taxes; those for obtaining food stamps; those that provide benefits to single mothers; those to obtain public housing; and many others. In all these cases, because of the gradual increase in the number of users, the costs of the programs will rise only gradually, with the passing of time. Programs that, when they were first introduced, may have seemed inexpensive and easily affordable by the government will gradually become a greater burden for the public accounts. Examples of this trend can be found in almost any country. A few purely illustrative examples are provided below.

The first example comes from the recent (2011), entertaining, and informative book, *Boomerang*, by Michael Lewis, on the Great Recession. Addressing the high cost of pensions in Greece at the time when he wrote the book, Lewis wrote (on p. 45):

> The retirement age for Greek jobs [that are] classified as *arduous* is as early as fifty five for men and fifty for women. As this is also the moment when the state begins to shovel out generous pensions, more than six hundred Greek professions [sic] [have] somehow managed [over the years] to get themselves classified as *arduous*: hairdressers, radio announcers, waiters, musicians, and on and on.

Therefore, most Greek workers had been able to retire at a relatively young age and get pensions that were almost as high as their final wages. Greece must, indeed, have been a very arduous and demanding, country to live in, before recent reforms forced by the crisis were made! From Lewis's description it becomes clear why the recent reforms in Greece attracted so much antagonism from groups of citizens.

A second good example comes from the United States. In 1939, while the Great Depression was still a reality, President F. D. Roosevelt initiated a program that allowed the *poorest* Americans to get food stamps from the Federal government. The food stamps allowed these *very poor* individuals to buy, with the use of the food stamps, basic food items. The program was clearly intended to be limited to the relatively few families that were considered *the poorest*. Over the years the food that could be obtained with the food stamps became less essential and less basic, and there were reports about food stamps being traded and ending up being used to buy alcoholic beverages for some individuals. Furthermore, and more directly relevant to our point, the number of qualifying individuals grew dramatically, even though the United States had come out of the Great Depression and had become a very rich country. Clearly the concept of poverty, and the definition of who should be considered poor, was being progressively adjusted with time. Persons that, given their absolute, real income may have been relatively well to do in 1939, in recent years were considered poor. According to a report by the US Congressional Budget Office, by the year 2011, the individuals who were getting food stamps, had reached 45 million, or one in every seven American, at a cost that had reached $72 billion. In the city of Washington, DC, a city with one of the highest per capita incomes in the world, and with a low unemployment rate, one in every five inhabitants, in 2011, was receiving food stamps. Since 2007, the number of beneficiaries from the food stamps, supposedly a program of assistance to the *very* poor, had grown by 70 percent.

Another American example comes from the enormous and progressive growth in coverage that came over the years in a program aimed at assisting *single women with dependent children*. This program was initiated, by F. D. Roosevelt, in 1935, also during the Great Depression. It had been intended to help *widowed women with small children*, at a time when there were no other programs to assist these women, and no pensions for the families of workers who died for whatever reason. The fact that dangerous jobs, especially for men, were then still common, as well as various illnesses, created a clearly defined and highly deserving group of potential beneficiaries from this program, specifically *poor widows who were left with small children*.

With the passing of time the requirements to benefit from this program became progressively less stringent. The women with small children no longer needed to be *widows*. They could be unmarried single women who had had children out of wedlock. The children no longer needed to be minor, or to have had a recognized father. The women could have relations and children with different men, as long as they did not marry the (living) fathers of their children, thus creating an incentive not to marry and to have more children. And there could be several fathers and several children from different fathers within a household. The more children a single woman had, the greater the public benefits she would receive, which included also medical care, food stamps, access to public housing, and some others.

Over several decades, this program created a situation whereby there were households in which no members had ever worked, for two or three generations. They had just accumulated children and had lived on the public benefits. The program created a psychology of dependency on government assistance, and the benefits received came to be seen as entitlements. It also created pressures on the government to increase the benefits. It developed classic cases of "poverty traps" because a woman that accepted a job lost in benefits perhaps more than she might earn in the job. Thus the implicit marginal tax rate on income from work was very high for these single women.

The program's costs grew enormously until 1995, when President Clinton, delivered, against sharp criticism from some directions, on a promise that he had made during the presidential campaign, "to end welfare as we know it." He tightened dramatically the benefits and established a time limit during which the benefits could be obtained (see Tanzi, 2011a, pp. 119–23). This Clinton reform, which was made possible by the fact that the Republicans were at that time controlling Congress, has been recognized has having been an important and successful one in the United States. Surely there must be other programs for which similar reforms are possible. The Clinton reform is important because it indicates that with enough political will the clock can be set backward to bring the programs back to their original intentions.

The disability pension programs of many countries provide other good examples of this law of growing public spending, because the concept of disability in a modern society is a highly flexible one. In many countries the number of disabled persons has grown enormously, making the disability programs very expensive, and giving the impression that the number of truly disabled persons in modern societies has grown dramatically over the years in spite of the better living conditions. This increase in numbers has occurred in spite of the fact that many of the occupations that in the past contributed to disabilities among workers have disappeared or have become much less important. What changed in many countries is not the *number* of true disabled persons but the *definition* of who is disabled. That definition became more flexible and liberal with the passing of time. Many individuals that in the past would have been considered to be in relatively good physical conditions managed to convince the relevant authorities that they were no longer able to work and, therefore, qualified for disability pensions.

In the United States the Social Security's *Disability* Insurance program was created in 1956, for all the workers who qualified for Social Security. It has been little changed since its creation. Many "states" and "counties" in the US also introduced similar programs for their public workers. The cost of these disability programs at the beginning was modest. Then the number of applications for disability retirement started to grow at a fast pace. Since 2007, that number had grown by 30 percent in 2011. By 2011, the cost of the Social Security's disability program had reached $212 billions, including $80 billions for medical assistance for which those qualifying for disability pensions become automatically eligible. The cost was $124 billion excluding the medical assistance costs. The average payment per month for beneficiaries was $1111 but adding the medical benefits it reached about $1500 per month. In 2011 there were 10 million beneficiaries, or about 4.5 percent of the working-age population. In 1970 only 1.3 percent of the working age population was considered disabled. The cost in 2011 was nine times what it was in 1970.

It has been estimated that the disability program will exhaust the trust fund accumulated to finance the expenses of the program, by 2016. As an expert who has studied this Federal program in detail put it: "the program's expenditure on cash transfers and medical benefits... are extremely high and growing unsustainably." Furthermore, "there is no compelling evidence... that the incidence of disabling conditions among the US working age population is rising" (see Autor, 2011, p. 1; Autor and Duggan, 2003). Obviously, the increase in the number of beneficiaries has not been due to an increase of the number of disabled persons, as that concept had originally been defined, but mainly to changing and more liberal definitions of disability.

In 1984 Congress changed the rules that defined whether a person is disabled. The definition was changed from specific objective conditions to an individual's general, medical condition. It was a process similar to the one that had happened with food stamps and with the assistance to single women' programs. The qualifying conditions for workers changed significantly over the years, from serious work accidents, incapacitating strokes, heart attacks, cancer, and similar causes, during working age, conditions that were easily identifiable, and thus controllable for veracity, by the authorities that had to make the decisions, to ailments such as mental problems, depression and personality disorders, back pain, joint stress and other such ailments, that are far less ascertainable and controllable. Some or many individuals saw the disability insurance as an alternative to work and once they started on disability, going to work implied a large marginal tax because they would lose their pension rights. The number of individuals who applied for disability pensions went up sharply after the recent crisis started.

The role of lawyers, and especially of representatives of labor unions, in pushing the claims for potential beneficiaries, has also been important. The lawyers have strong incentives to do the pushing, because they get a significant share of the money that claimants may receive to cover past claims, when the lawyers succeed in getting approvals for their clients. Of course, the labor unions have always an almost Pavlovian bias, in siding with the workers that they represent and in expanding their presumed rights. Because the growth in spending was progressive over the years, it did not generate strong reactions to stop it and checks on the disabled were progressively reduced.

As already mentioned, in the United States the local governments have also their own disability pension programs for their public employees. An interesting illustration of our *law of expanding public spending* has been the program of disability pensions for police officers in Montgomery County, a jurisdiction in Maryland, just outside Washington, DC. This county has one of the highest average incomes among all counties in the United States. A large and increasing number of the police officers of this county have managed, over the years, to claim disability pensions for very slight injuries, including the claim of sore elbow. These police officers have been able to retire, at relatively young ages, years before the official retirement age. Until 2012 they had been able to retire with 70 percent of their final salary, but with a pension income that was free of taxes. After retiring, they could often get other jobs, without losing their disability pensions.

It should not be surprising that almost half of all the police officers that left the Montgomery County police force in recent years had done so taking advantage of this generous "disability pension" opportunity. The Montgomery County Police Department apparently was full of "disabled persons." This program contributed to create increasing fiscal problems for the public accounts of this rich county. Pressures for reform had been resisted until 2012, by politicians who were afraid to lose the votes of the well-organized labor union of the police officers. Finally, in 2012, because of growing fiscal problems for the county and growing public pressures, a law was passed that made a distinction between those with *serious* disabilities and those with *minor* ones, a difference that still depended on distinctions that were not easy to make. Those who now retire with minor disabilities will get lower pensions. This law will reduce but not eliminate the problem. Political resistance from the labor union made it difficult for the policymakers of Montgomery County to be more courageous and to introduce more substantive changes. Still this could be seen as an other example of the possibility of stopping or reducing the growth of public spending.

Similar stories have been reported for several European and other countries. In some countries, such as the Netherlands, large shares of the population had been defined as disabled over the years and as such had been entitled to public pensions. However, in the Netherlands, reforms in recent years were able to dramatically reduce the new disability cases. In some countries the need to assist relatives who are disabled may also entitle some individuals to benefit from disability pensions. In Italy, for example, some relatively young individuals have been allowed to retire, presumably to take care of parents with disabilities. According to news reports some of these individuals had immediately gone to work in other jobs, without losing the disability pension. There have also been reports of abuses such as presumably blind retirees that were discovered driving trucks, or of people receiving disability pensions because they were unable to walk, who were observed playing soccer. The problem is obviously often compounded by corruption.

In a recent study of a proposed new National Disability Insurance Scheme in Australia (see Baker, 2012) the author has concluded that the scheme "will be a monster of a government program. It will start big and get bigger, and grow to become the new leviathan of the Australian welfare state." The author adds that the government's cost estimates have been revised upward regularly and that estimates of the eligible population have also changed.

In a book published some years ago, on the growth of public spending in Italy, an economist at the Bank of Italy described in considerable detail how the regular pension expenditure had grown, because of a process similar to the one described above for disability pensions (see Franco, 1993). The right to getting pensions had been progressively stretched to cover individuals other than the direct and immediate beneficiaries of the original pension system. Similar descriptions have been reported for other countries, including the United States. In the United States some women ended up with multiple pensions, obtained from having married several times, after getting divorces, and having stayed married to each husband the minimum amount of time required to entitle them to the pension, to which the husband had a claim. Frequently, the pension rights of the workers who had contributed to the payments of social security taxes have been extended to persons that bear some relationship to the worker, through marriage or some other relation.

As an interesting current example, regardless of the intrinsic merit of this controversial legal change, defining same-sex unions as legal marriages will make many individuals entitled to receive some government benefits, including pension rights and medical assistance, that in the past had been claimed by only one of the partners in the relationship. In other cases still, in some countries, systems have developed whereby, in some government institutions, individuals are systematically promoted just a short time before they reach the retirement age. This allows them to increase the amount of the pension received, when that amount depends on the most recent salary.

The above are all expressions of what we have called a fundamental, and almost universal, law, of how and why public spending tends to grow with the passing of time, even in the absence of major legislative changes, because, what could be considered, free riders, or perhaps less-deserving beneficiaries, are added to the list of beneficiaries of government programs. Only specific reforms, or a determined effort on the part of governments, as we have seen in some programs, can put a stop to this growth. But governments that try to do so risk paying a political price when those who are negatively affected are able to organize politically.

In 1995, in the United States, President Clinton managed to put a stop to the welfare program for single women with dependent children, because of a lucky combination of circumstances. Some other countries, including Sweden, managed to do it with more comprehensive reforms. There is scope for reducing public spending in most countries by restricting the abuses and reversing some trends, but to do so requires a kind of tough love that has not been common in most countries in recent decades. It requires also the recognition that the resources that the government uses are never truly free resources and that governments cannot solve all the people's problems but must focus on the fundamental ones in which they have a chance of success. When that focus is lost, growing problems follow.

Let us now go to the second reason for the existence of the fundamental law of the growth in public spending. Often, the benefits or the services provided by governments to citizens, through particular social programs, have expanded in scope after they were introduced, leading to an increase in the number of public employees that deliver the services and, of course, to the cost of the services. Thus the increase in the cost of some public programs may be due not to the increase in the numbers of *users* of the services, as we saw above, but to the increase in the *providers* of the services.

In public schools, or in public health services, or in some other services, the number of public employees who are paid to provide the services to the citizens, and the costs of providing them, increase because of the gradual addition of administrators, consultants, specialists, advisors, managers, and others, to the public payroll. Some of these additions may be required by technological changes, as in medical practices, or by more stringent reporting requirements. Some are not. Even when technology may explain the additions, they do not always legitimize its use. For example, as mentioned earlier, there are new, very expensive drugs that can prolong the lives of some patients by a few months. Should a public health service pay for them when the resources might be used far more productively in other uses? Some of these drugs cost hundreds of thousands of dollars per year and per patient. Should the fact that public health systems pay for these drugs, or for some health procedures, lead to the conclusion that the cost to society is zero or should be ignored? Does something become affordable only because it is the state that pays for it?

In the United States' public schools the number of employees who deal with the provision of lunches and other services to the students, or with sport-related and other social activities (activities that have little to do with the provision of education, as strictly defined), or the number of child psychologists or other special activities' professionals, to deal with children who are considered to have particular learning or behavioral problems, has grown significantly over the years, in addition to the growth of the general administrators. It is often difficult to control these changes and easy to advance strong justifications to justify them. For example the number of administrators that deal with "diversity issues" has grown as has the number of employees that deal with problem children. The assumption that no student should be left behind is a strong motivation for the hiring of these individuals.

The individuals who benefit from government programs *as providers* (individuals who often enjoy more job security and better working conditions than they would in private sector jobs) grow with the passage of time, often leading to significant increases in the costs of the programs. In several countries, the benefits received by public employees and their fiscal costs have increased at a much faster pace than in the private sector. In some cases the benefits that these individuals convey have been strongly questioned.

A third reason for the progressive growth of public spending, is the growing *inefficiency* that develops over time in publicly financed programs that provide services, including those of public enterprises. Public railroads, post offices, public airlines, and other similar activities are especially subjected to this problem. The inefficiency, or the fat, that contributes to higher public spending over the years, is the normal one accumulated by institutions that often find themselves in positions of monopoly, and that do not face the pressures to reduce costs that private enterprises experience in competitive markets. Job tenure for public workers contributes significantly to the growing public sector inefficiency. If an employee cannot be fired, regardless of performance, he or she is less likely to give all the effort to the tasks to be performed.

The connection between job tenure, strongly defended by labor unions, and poor performance and inefficiency in US public schools has attracted a lot of media attention in recent years. See, for example, the award-winning documentary *Waiting for Superman*, which provides startling examples of inefficiency in some US public school systems. These inefficiencies lead to low returns for the money spent in some programs. Attempts to reduce inefficiency in some school systems (as for example those of Washington, DC, and New York) have not been very successful so far. The sad part is that some of the school systems that spend the most per student are among the least efficient. In Italy the differences in efficiency among the health systems of different regions, and also among their educational systems, are significant and well known and they do not depend on differences in the financial resources available to the different regions. Recently, startling examples, of the differences in the efficiency of regional governments have also been documented.

Other American examples of the possibly unnecessary growth of public spending, examples that it is a bit difficult to place in any of the categories provided above, have come out, recently, as a side product of General Petraeus' scandal and resignation and, separately, from statistics on employees of universities. Several news reports have described the lavish and expensive lifestyle enjoyed by generals in the US army, as well as the inflation that had taken place over the years in the number of American generals. The ratio of high-level officials to enlisted soldiers has gone up dramatically over the years. This expansion has also been reported in other countries. Furthermore, and perhaps with greater implications for public spending, many high-ranking military officers retire at relatively young ages and immediately go to work for the same defense industry enterprises with which they had been dealing, while they were in their military jobs. Their role in the enterprises is often that of facilitating or pushing the contracts with the Pentagon on new weapons systems. This has had the effect of making the Pentagon buy far more weapons and, perhaps, also less suitable weapons than it should. These revolving-door positions have contributed to keeping the defense budget far more expensive than it needs to be to achieve the true defense objectives of the country. When the Pentagon announces a reduction in its spending, the complaint is often that the reduction will cut jobs in particular states as if the creation of jobs were the objective of defense spending. Unfortunately these revolving-door actions have also spread to other areas, especially some regulatory areas, with similar effects on public spending.

It has been reported that in the past couple of decades the employment of administrators in American universities has increased at a rate that was ten times faster than that of tenured professors. The teaching part of universities seems to have become much less important than it used to be. Furthermore the salaries of an increasing number of high-level US university administrators have reached very high levels, some as high as millions of dollars. Taxpayers often have to meet these higher costs, either through taxes or through higher tuition fees for their children.

Another, non-American, example, on how costs can go up in public institutions may be provided by the IMF, the institution with which the author of this book was associated for 27 years. When the author first joined the IMF, in 1974, there was one person that dealt with external relations and this person seemed to spend an unusual amount of time in the IMF coffee shop, because he had little to do. By the time the author of this book left the IMF, in 2000, there was a whole department dealing with external relations, and the size and importance of that department seems to have grown further in more recent years. This expansion may have been justified by the need to be more transparent and to provide more information to the world, in other words by the need to add an additional objective to the functions of the institution. However, adding additional objectives is always costly in resources and it might also be considered by some a sign of growing inefficiency. Perhaps the staff increase was required to accommodate growing demands on institutions such as the IMF, to promote more transparency. In any case, the result has been to increase the resources needed by that organization. Often it is not realized that growing demands for more transparency, for more diversity, or for more control from the top, can have significant cost implications. As these demands increase over the years, they lead to increased costs for many government programs.

In studying government programs, it is easy to find remarkable examples of the growth of public spending due to some of the reasons described in this study. In some systems public employees, who are often absent from their work places, are common. Some may be away on vacation using sick leave. There have even been some reports about real "ghost workers," workers that exist only on the payrolls. In some public systems the public employees are present but it is almost the same as if they were ghost workers, because they do little productive work and still occupy space and use resources. One is reminded of an observation, made a century ago by Vilfredo Pareto, the famous Italian economist, when public spending was still a low share of GDP. Pareto commented that in most public offices, 20 percent of the employees often did 80 percent of the productive work. Some of the inefficiencies may originate from work rules promoted by labor unions; some by the widening of objectives that most programs must satisfy; others are just the result of lax controls, or of the view that when it is the government that pays, nobody pays, so that it is not necessary to give one's full effort.

In many countries the *fundamental law of public expenditure growth* has been largely responsible for making the share of public spending into GDPs grow over the years, *after* the time when the countries first introduced the legislation that made them welfare states. Therefore, part of the blame for the growth of spending should not be assigned to the original legislation, or even to the original programs, but to the lax controls and additional demands that followed it. It may be possible, though clearly difficult, to bring the welfare states a long way back to *their original versions,* an action which, if successful, would significantly reduce public spending. Sweden, Canada, and some other countries have, to some extent and with considerable success, managed to do this.

The current crisis might give the governments the excuse and the justification to attempt to do what was suggested above. Some evidence indicates that some movement in this direction may have started, in some European countries. However, there is a long way for the countries to go, and there remains the danger that the still limited and half-hearted recent reforms might be cancelled, by future, populist governments, that will use the arguments that some economists have been making, that to get out of the crisis it is necessary to spend more not less. It might not be too difficult to convince an electorate that has little knowledge of economics that with enough spending countries can get out of all crises.

# 15
# Concluding Remarks

In this study we have argued that the difficulties that the EMU countries have been experiencing have had less to do with the use of the common currency, the euro, or even with the characteristics of the European Monetary Union, and a lot to do with the levels to which public spending was pushed over the years combined with limited and inefficient controls on banks and on the financial system. These developments made it easier for countries to finance large public spending until concerns about the sustainability of their fiscal accounts started to affect borrowing costs. For example the purchase by Cypriot banks of Greek government bonds made it easier for Greece to expand its public spending and in turn created problems for Cyprus. In most of the countries of the EMU, but also in other countries including the United States, with the help of foreign loans, public spending had been pushed to levels that, sooner or later, would become unsustainable and lead to potential fiscal crises.

The 2008 financial crisis had simply anticipated when that time would come. If the euro were to disappear tomorrow, the problems of several of the EMU countries would, in all likelihood, become more difficult to deal with, rather than less difficult as some observers continue to believe. The problem has not been the existence of the euro but the countries' policies.

The main problem facing many countries is that the level of public spending that was legislated and established over past years became progressively more difficult to finance, either with higher tax revenue or with more borrowed funds, especially funds borrowed domestically. Unless changes are made, the current spending levels will become even more difficult to finance in future years. In many countries, over the years taxes were pushed to levels where they met strong resistance from taxpayers. This made it difficult, politically or administratively, to keep raising the tax levels. This obstacle shifted the attention of the policymakers from taxes to public borrowing. Public borrowing increased sharply over the years, making the ratios of public debts to GDPs rise significantly. But, once again, in an increasing number of countries it started to encounter the resistance of creditors, which led to increasing costs of borrowing for some countries.

Many countries accumulated enormous public debts and exposed themselves not only to high financing costs in order to service the official public debts, but also to huge future unfunded liabilities, that in many countries are far higher than the official public debts. The already very high explicit public debts, reported by the statistics, do not include the unfunded liabilities and other contingent liabilities that have been assumed implicitly or explicitly by governments. These may include the need to recapitalize banks in difficulties. Therefore, the official statistics tend to give a rosier picture of the forthcoming reality. The truth is that assuming that current policies do not change, the fiscal situation in many industrial countries, and not just in EMU countries, is far worse than reported.

Those who continue to call for higher public spending, presumably "to promote growth" that would make the unemployment rate fall and the economies grow at faster rates, are playing with fire, by giving dangerous advice to policymakers and by creating populist expectations that there is a free lunch provided by a choice between unpleasant austerity and easy and comfortable growth. In some cases this is the equivalent of giving snake oil to patients that are seriously ill.

A permanent solution to the crisis will inevitably require significant reductions in current public spending and reductions in future commitments tied to entitlements or to expectations of government rescues of banks and other institutions. This reduction obviously cannot be achieved over night. In some countries, such as the US and Japan, it is likely to require also some increase in taxes, because of the high debts and the comparatively low tax burdens. The reductions in current public spending, as several countries have discovered, must be made even if such a reduction might, for a while, lead to increased unemployment and reduction in economic activity.

This temporary reduction in activity inevitably leads to criticism, by convinced Keynesians and by those who benefit directly from government programs. However, without such reduction, several countries will experience a continuation of precarious economic conditions prone to crises, and situations in which interest rates on public debts might rise dangerously, because of perceptions that lending to these countries has become riskier; or because of a return to expectations of the high inflations that often characterized similar situations in the past. Several EMU countries experienced the danger of fast-growing interest rates on their borrowing in the recent crisis years.

It should be reiterated that the reduction in public spending by high-spending countries should not require the destruction of the original welfare systems created in the past, as some observers fear. It should not require the destruction of genuine and basic safety nets for the most deserving citizens. It requires that government spending becomes more focused and more efficient in its effects, recognizing that resources are scarce, whether used collectively, by the state, or privately, by individuals. In some sense resources have become scarcer after the Great Recession, because the recession has lowered the future growth rates of many economies.

A strategy aimed at improving permanently and in an equitable way the European and other countries' public accounts requires not more spending, or the creation of a fiscal union, but the explicit recognition of the *fundamental law of the growth in public spending* described in the previous chapter. It requires first stopping and then reversing the effects of that law, that over the years had made public spending move on an escalator that went only upward, in spite of the fact that markets were becoming more efficient and more capable of offering private alternatives to public spending, for the satisfaction of some social needs and for protection against some risks (see Tanzi, 2005). The recognition of that law could go a long way toward making governments more efficient, and fiscal accounts more sustainable. It would require setting the clock back by a few decades and attempting to return the public programs' coverage, scope, and efficiency as close as possible to the original intentions of the legislators, when the programs were first introduced.

It would definitely require a change of attitude by both policymakers and citizens, and a healthy dose of skepticism, *vis-à-vis* many of the actions by governments that require additional public spending. This does not mean that the essential role of the government in modern societies should be reduced. It would recognize that governments cannot protect all the citizens against all the risks, but only some citizens against some risks.

A "nanny state" often encourages many citizens to shift to the government the responsibility for dealing with some risks which many of them could deal with directly. A "nanny state" creates poverty traps for individuals who could work but who find it more convenient not to work because of the support that they may get from their governments. It is important for citizens to recognize that resources are always scarce, and that the function of governments should be to prevent hell on earth, rather than to try to establish heaven. When the state tries to do too many things, it inevitably brings excessive complexity in its actions and becomes inefficient. This has happened to many countries.

This change of course and of attitude will require time, determination and technical work; however, the process of making governments work more efficiently than they have been so far cannot wait until the situation returns to normal. That time might never come. To a limited extent, and in spite of the obvious difficulties, and often in the face of strong opposition and criticism, the change of course has started in some countries. But doubts remain whether that process would be maintained in the future and not reversed by changes of governments and by populist opposition.

The scope for cutting public spending in some countries is clearly indicated by the large differences (differences as large as 10, 20, or even 30, percentage points of GDP) that now exist between the levels of public spending among some industrial countries, and also by the already-mentioned experiences of countries that, in the past couple decades, did succeed in cutting that spending by large percentages. Compare, for example, the level of public spending as a share of GDP in Australia, Korea, Japan, Taiwan, Singapore, and Switzerland on one hand, with that of Belgium, France, Italy and some other countries, on the other hand.

A remarkable and surprising discovery in the above comparison is that the large differences in public spending, between these two groups, do not seem to be associated with equivalent differences in the wellbeing that governments provide, or aim to provide, to their citizens, at least as measured by the effects of public spending on important socio-economic indicators. Public spending is supposed to improve a country's socio-economic indicators, indicators that increase the welfare of the countries' citizens. However, it often does not do it. (For statistical evidence of this affirmation see Afonso *et al.*, 2010; Tanzi, 2011a.)

The governments of Australia and Switzerland seem to provide as good socio-economic indicators, and as good public welfare, as those of France, Italy, or other high-spending countries, even though they spend much less, as shares of their GDPs. On the contrary the lower-spending countries often show better results, in generating desirable socio-economic indicators and also better macroeconomic outcomes (see Tanzi, 2011a).

Through much observation of the performance of countries, over almost half a century, the author of this book has become convinced that, in general, with a level of public spending of, say, 30 to 35 percent of GDP, governments should be able to satisfy all the collective wants that they can satisfy effectively and efficiently. Public spending levels beyond 35 percent of GDP normally bring about inefficiency, fiscal churning, complexity in policies, and problems of horizontal inequity among citizens, because undeserving individuals end up getting benefits equal to those of deserving ones. Several countries now spend 10 or more percent of GDP above the above limits. Of course, this level of spending is not necessarily "optimal" in some theoretical sense. It is not based on any specific or grand theory. It can, therefore, be easily criticized. However, it is a level based on concrete observations and experience (see, Tanzi, 2011a; Tanzi and Schuknecht, 2000). It could be added that for countries that are more efficient in using public resources, and where there is more of a community spirit among the population (as for example there seems to be in Scandinavian countries), the limit could be higher than for countries where this spirit is less pronounced. However the problem of increasing complexity, that accompanies higher levels of public spending, would remain a concern.

When faced with major economic crises, some countries have managed in the recent past to reduce the levels of their public spending by truly remarkable amounts. This was especially the case in the welfare states of Northern Europe and in Canada, but also in the Netherlands, New Zealand, and some other countries. Sweden is today seen as a highly successful country, with a healthy and growing economy. However, it is still a welfare state, but a more efficient and sustainable one than it was 20 years ago. Canada was a big spender in the early 1990s, with a large fiscal deficit and a fast-growing public debt. In the mid 1990s a government with clear ideas, and strong political determination to control public spending, started making major reforms that had, in part, the objective of making the clock move backward. Both of these countries did not change the basic or fundamental objectives that previous governments had set for the citizens. They were and still are seen as "welfare states," but they are surely more efficient welfare states than they used to be. They tried to stop and reverse the effects on public spending that we have attributed to our law of expanding public sector cost. Tough love was enough to make a real difference. The Australian and Swiss experiences, with their much lower level of public spending, but with high levels of socio-economic indicators, suggest that Sweden and Canada may even have more scope for (efficient and fair) expenditure reduction, should they wish to continue pursuing this course.

Countries such as France and Italy could surely go a long way on this road, because, with all the talk about austerity, they still spend more than 50 percent of their GDPs in public expenditure, and have extraordinarily high tax burdens that have even been increased recently. In Italy areas for major expenditure reductions are common and clearly visible to any sophisticated observer. However, significant expenditure reductions would not only require "spending reviews," as they were introduced in 2012 by the Monti government, but also what the author of this book has called a change in the *architecture* of the public sector. That architecture has to do with the number of members of parliament, the number of municipalities, the too many layers of governments in the federal system, with the limited controls on the expenditures of sub-national governments, with cultural aspects of public life, that require huge buildings, thousands of official cars, and so on (see Tanzi, 2011c, for some examples).

At this time (early 2013) it is difficult to tell whether the euro will survive or not, as it is difficult to tell whether the dollar, the pound or the yen will survive as solid currencies. The latest news suggests that the early demise of the euro, predicted repeatedly by some economists, was much exaggerated. It seems more likely than not that the euro will survive the current and possibly future crises of which there will inevitably be some. At the same time the current crisis may have brought a stronger sense of unity within those who make the basic decisions within EMU. It may be less certain whether the composition of the countries that are now part of the European Monetary System will necessarily remain unchanged in the future, but again the best guess at this time is that it probably will and that the number of countries in the EMU may even continue to grow.

The survival of the euro over the longer run, and the economic performance of the European and also of other countries, will depend more on the depth, efficiency and fairness of the reforms that the *individual* countries will be able to make than on collective reforms, although some such reforms, aimed at strengthening the single market, as for example the recent creation of a single bank regulator, may be important. The reforms made individually by the countries will need to bring the public spending to a comfortable and more easily sustainable level, and probably will have to include some effective and well-enforced rules on fiscal deficits and on public debts, and perhaps also on the level of public spending.

Some non-euro countries, such as the US the UK, and Japan will need to follow similar roads, to prevent their getting into crises as serious or more serious as those now affecting some of the EMU countries. The UK government seems to have understood this need, so far, better than the US or the Japanese policymakers.

It is not likely that the euro problem, if there is such a problem, as some observers believe, would be solved by the creation of a "European Fiscal, or Transfer, Union," one that would redistribute large amounts of money from some member countries to other countries in difficulties. The creation of a European Federation, and of a European Federal Government, with large powers to tax and to spend, might be desirable for many reasons not discussed in this book, and at some time in the future might become a desirable outcome, to better deal with European-wide public goods. Examples of such goods could be European defense, European-wide infrastructures, basic research, dealing with immigration and environmental problems, and perhaps also for bringing more uniformity to the welfare programs and tax systems that continue to be widely divergent among the countries. However, it is less likely that it would be useful to solve this or future fiscal crises. In the US the fiscal union (the Federal government) has simply pushed the deficit and the public debt problem upward, to the US Federal government. It has not contained it.

Finally, before Christmas of 2012 when the writing of this book was being brought to an end, the news reports, while still revealing worries about the Mayan calendar's prediction of the imminent end of the world, seemed less concerned about the end of the euro than they had been. The value of the euro had risen sharply to a seven-month high against the dollar, surely not an endorsement of the dollar or a prediction of the early demise of the euro; a hedge fund had made a $500 million gain on a bet that the euro would survive; the rating agency Standard & Poor's had raised the credit rating of Greece by several notches, allowing Greek sovereign debt to become again eligible, at the ECB, as collateral for its funding operations; the spreads for Spain and Italy had fallen sharply; and the professional euro-skeptics, those who question the survival of the euro and of the EMU had been left with a rich source of speculation as to whether the end of the world, or the collapse of the EMU system, would come first. Also recently, the ratings of UK and even Chinese debt have come into question.

The recent developments in Cyprus and the Italian elections have brought back some excitement and have heightened the need to worry about the level of the public spending and the regulation of the financial market. These remain the key areas of policy to watch. The Cyprus experience has shown that banks should not be protected when they act irresponsibly and make possible for other countries (read Greece) to spend more than they should. To conclude, as one of the founders of the European Union (Jean Monnet) put it a long time ago: "Europe will be forged in crises and will be the sum of the solutions adopted for those crises." It should not be forgotten that the European Monetary System is less than two decades old and that its creation was a very complex enterprise. All complex projects need corrections until they are made to work well. It took more than two centuries for that other project, that other monetary union that is the United States of America. In those two centuries many mistakes made at its creation had to be corrected and some are still being corrected.

# References

Admati, Anat and Martin Hellwig (2013) *The Bankers' New Clothes* (Princeton University Press).

Afonso, A., L. Schuknecht and V. Tanzi (2010) "Public Sector Efficiency: Evidence for New EU Member States and Emerging Markets," *Applied Economics*, **42** (17), 2147–64.

Alesina, Alberto (2012) "Cut Deficits by Cutting Spending," *Vox*, 12 November.

Alesina, Alberto and Francesco Giavazzi (eds) (2012) *Fiscal Policy after the Financial Crisis* (Chicago: University of Chicago Press).

Alesina, Alberto and Roberto Perotti (1997) "The Welfare State and Competitiveness," *American Economic Review*, **87** (5), 921–39.

Alesina, Alberto and Silvia Ardagna (2010) "Large Changes in Fiscal Policy: Taxes versus Spending," in Jeffrey R. Brown (ed.), *Tax Policy and Economy*, vol. 24 (University of Chicago Press).

Ali Abbas, S. M. *et al.* (2010) "Strategies for Fiscal Consolidation in the Post-Crisis World" (Washington, DC: IMF Fiscal Affairs Department).

Almunia, Joaqin (2006) "Fiscal Discipline and the Reform of the Stability and Growth Pact," in National Bank of Poland, *Fiscal Policy and the Road to the Euro* (Warsaw).

Ardagna, Silvia (2004) "Fiscal Stabilizations: When Do They Work and Why?," *European Economic Review*, **48** (5), 1047–74.

Arrow, Kenneth J. (1974) *The Limits of Organization* (New York: Norton).

Aslund, Anders and Marek Dabrowski (2007) *Europe After Enlargement* (Cambridge University Press).

Auerbach, Alan and Yuriy Gorodnichenko (2012) "Fiscal Multipliers in Recessionand Expansion," in Alberto Alesina and Francesco Giavazzi (eds), *Fiscal Policy after the Financial Crisis* (University of Chicago Press).

Autor, David H. (2011) "The Unsustainable Rise of the Disability Rolls in the United States: Causes, Consequences, and Policy Options," unpublished paper, 23 November.

Autor, David H. and Mark G. Duggan (2003) "The Rise in the Disability Rolls and the Decline in Unemployment," *Quarterly Journal of Economics*, **118** (1), 157–205.

Baker, Andrew (2012), "The New Leviathan: A National Disability Insurance Scheme," The Centre for Independent Studies (Australia), CIS Policy Monographs 131.

Baldacci, E. and M. S. Kumar (2010) "Fiscal Deficits, Debt and Interest Rates," IMF Working Paper 10/184.

Banca D'Italia (2012) *Rules and Institutions for Sound Fiscal Policy after the Crisis* (Rome), no. 11.

Baumol, William J. (1967) "Macroeconomics of Unbalanced Growth: The Anatomy of Urban Crisis," *American Economic Review,* **57** (3), 415–26.

Blanchard, Olivier and Daniel Leigh (2013) "Growth: Forecast Errors and Fiscal Multipliers," IMF Working Paper 13/1 (January).

Blanchard, Olivier, Giovanni Dell'Ariccia and Paola Mauro (2013) "Rethinking Macro Policy II: Getting Granular," *IMF Staff Discussion Note,* SDN/13/03 (April 2013).

Blinder, Alan (2012) *After the Music Stopped: The Financial Crisis, the Response, and the Work Ahead* (New York: Penguin).

Brixi, Hana Polackova, and Allen Schick (2002) *Government at Risk* (Washington, DC: World Bank).

Brooks, Richard (2013) *The Great Tax Robbery* (Oneworld).

Buti, Marco, Servaas Deroose, Vitor Gaspar, and Joao Nogueira Martins (eds) (2010) *The Euro: The First Decade* (Cambridge University Press).

Canzoneri, Matthew B., Vittorio Grilli, and Paul Masson (eds) (1992) *Establishing a Central Bank: Issues in Europe and Lessons from the USA* (Cambridge University Press).

Cecchetti, Stephen G., M. S. Mohanty, and Fabrizio Zampolli (2010) "The Future of Public Debt: Prospects and Implications," BIS Working Papers no. 300.

Cecchetti, Stephen G., Robert N. McCauley, and Patrick M. McGuire (2012) "Interpreting TARGET2 Balances," BIS Working Papers no. 393 (December).

Chinn, Menzil (2012) "Fiscal Multipliers" in *The New Palgrave Dictionary of Economics* (forthcoming).

Coenen, G., R. Straub and M. Trabandt (2012) "Fiscal Policy and the Great Recession in the Euro Area," ECB Working Paper Series no. 1429 (March).

Congress of the United States (2012) *The 2012 Long-Term Budget Outlook* (Washington, DC: June).

Corsetti, Giancarlo (ed.) (2012) *Austerity: Too Much of a Good Thing?* (London: Centre for Economic Policy Research).

Cottarelli, Carlo and Laura Jaramillo (2012) "Walking Hand in Hand: Fiscal Policy and Growth in Advanced Economies," IMF Working Paper 12/137.

Cour-Thimann, Philippine (2012) "Target2 Balances in the Euro Area Crisis Context" (Frankfurt: European Central Bank, 16–17 July).

Courchene, Thomas J (2006) "Balanced Budgets: A Canadian Fiscal Value," paper presented at conference on "The Long-Term Budget Challenges: Public Finance and Fiscal Sustainability in the G7," Washington, DC (2–4 June).

de Mooij, Ruud and Michael Keen (2012) "Fiscal Devaluation and Fiscal Consolidation: the VAT in Troubled Times", *Working Paper 17913,* NBER.

DeLong, J. Bradford and Lawrence H. Summers (2012) "Fiscal Policy in a Depressed Economy," *Brookings Papers on Economic Activity, Spring 2012,* available at http://www.brookings.edu/~/media/Projects/BPEA/Spring%202012/2012a_DeLong.pdf.

Dornbusch, Rudiger (1989) "Comment," in Mario Monti (ed.), *Fiscal Policy, Economic Adjustment, and Financial Markets* (Washington, DC and

Milan: International Monetary Fund and Centro di Economia monetariae finanziaria).
EEAG (2010) "Fiscal Policy Reaction to the Cycle in OECD: Pro- or Countercyclical?," OECD, ECO Working Paper no. 763 (Paris, 19 May).
EEAG (2012) *The EEAG Report on the European Economy* (Munich: CESifo).
Egert, Balazs (2013) "Public Debt, Economic Growth and Nonlinear Effects – Myth or Reality?" CESifo Working Paper no. 4157 (March).
European Commission (annual) *Public Finances in EMU* (Brussels).
European Commission (2013), "European Economic Forecast, Winter 2013", *European Economy* (Brussels).
Eyraud. Luc and Anke Weber (2013) "The Challenge of Debt Reduction during Fiscal Consolidation," IMF Working Paper 13/6.
Feldstein, Martin (1997a) "EMU and International Conflict," *Foreign Affairs*, **76** (6), 60–73.
Feldstein, Martin (1997b) "The Political Economy of the European and Monetary Union: Political Sources of an Economic Liability," *Journal of Economic Perspectives*, **11** (4), 23–42.
Fels, Gerhard and George M. von Fursternberg (eds) (1989) *A Supply-Side Agenda for Germany* (Heidelberg: Springer).
Franco, Daniele (1993) *L'espansione della spesa publica in Italia* (Bologna: Il Mulino).
Friedman, Milton (1997) "Why Europe Can't Afford the Euro – The Danger of a Common Currency," *The Times*, 19 November.
Fröhlich, Hans-Peter (1989) "Supply-Side Policies in Germany: Economics Versus Politics," in Fels and von Fursternberg (eds).
Giavazzi, Francesco (2010) "The Stimulus Debate and the Golden Rule of Mountain Climbing," *Vox*, 22 July.
Giordano, R., *et al.* (2011) "The Public Sector Pay Gap in a Selection of Euro Area Countries," ECB Working Paper Series no. 1406 (December).
Gokhale, Jagadeesh (2013) *Spending Beyond our Means: How We Are Bankrupting Future Generations* (Washington, DC: CATO Institute).
Goldstein, Morris and Geoffrey Woglom (1992) "Market-Based Fiscal Discipline in Monetary Unions: Evidence from the US Municipal Bond Market," in M. Canzoneri, V. Grilli, and P. Masson (eds), *Establishing a Central Bank: Issues in Europe and Lessons from the United States* (Cambridge University Press).
Golinelli, R. and S. Momigliano (2008) "The Cyclical Response of Fiscal Policy in the Euro Area: Why do Results of Empirical Research Differ so Strongly?," Banca d'Italia Working Papers no. 654 (January).
Goodhart, Charles (1975) "Monetary Relationships: A View from Threadeedle Street," *Papers in Monetary Economics* (Canberra: Reserve Bank of Australia).
Greenlaw, David, John D. Hamilton, Peter Hooper, and Frederic S. Mishkin (2013) "Crunch Time: Fiscal crises and the Role of Monetary Policy," paper written for the US Monetary Policy Forum, New York City, 22 February.
Greenspan, Alan (2007) *The Age of Turbulence: Adventures in a New World* (New York: Penguin).

Hall, P. (ed.) (1989) *The Political Power of Economic Ideas: Keynesianism Across Nations* (Princeton University Press).

Horta Correia, Isabel (2011) "Fiscal Devaluation," *Banco de Portugal*, Article 27.

Hughes Hallett, Andrew and Juan Carlos Martinez Oliva (2013) "The Importance of Trade and Capital Imbalances in the European Debt Crisis," Peterson Institute for International Economics, Working Paper Series, WP 13-01 (January).

Hume, David (1955) *Writings on Economics*, ed. E. Rotuein (London: Nelson).

Ilzetzki, Ethan, Enrique Mendoza and Carlos A. Vegh (2013) "How Big (Small?) are Fiscal Multipliers?," *Journal of Monetary Economics* (forthcoming).

IMF (2012a) "Balancing Fiscal Policy Risks," *Fiscal Monitor* (April).

IMF (2012b) "Fiscal transparency, Accountability, and Risk," unpublished (7 August).

Irwin, Timothy C. (2012) "Accounting Devices and Fiscal Illusions," IMF Staff Discussion Note SDN/12/02 (Washington, DC, 28 March).

King, Mervyn (1992) "Discussion," in M. Canzoneri, V. Grilli, and P. Masson (eds), *Establishing a Central Bank: Issues in Europe and Lessons from the United States* (Cambridge University Press).

Koning, J. P. (2012) 'The Idiot's Guide to the Federal Reserve Interdistrict Settlement Account," blog (5February), http://jpkoning.blogspot.com/2012/02/idiots-guide-to-federal-reserve.htmi.

Kumar, M. and J. Woo (2010) "Public Debt and Growth," IMF Working Paper 10/174 (July).

Lamo, A., J. J. Perez, and L. Schuknecht (2011) "Public or Private Sector Leadership? An International Perspective," *Scandinavian Journal of Economics*, **114** (1), 228–44.

Larosière, Jacques de (1982) "The Growth of Public Debt and the Need for Fiscal Discipline," IMF pamphlet (Washington, DC).

Lewis, Michael (2010) *The Big Short: Inside the Doomsday Machine* (New York Norton).

Lewis, Michael (2011) *Boomerang: Travels in the New Third World* (New York: Norton).

Lindbeck, Assar (1995) "Hazardous Welfare State Dynamics," *American Economic Review, Papers and Proceedings*, **85** (2), 9–15.

Mauro, Paolo, Rafael Rameu, Ariel Binder, and Asad Zaman (2013) "A modern History of Fiscal Prudence and Profligacy," IMF Working Paper 13/5.

Mayer, Martin (1998) *The Bankers: The Next Generation* (New York: Truman Talley Books/Plume).

Mishkin, Frederic S. (various editions) *The Economics of Money, Banking, and Financial Markets*, (New York: HarperCollins).

Monti, Mario (ed.) (1989) *Fiscal Policy, Economic Adjustment, and Financial Markets* (Washington, DC and Milan: International Monetary Fund and Centro di Economia monetariae finanziaria).

Mueller, Dennis (2003) *Public Choice*, 3rd edn (Cambridge University Press).

Mundell, Robert A. (1961) "A Theory of Optimum Currency Areas," *American Economic Review*, **51** (4), 657–65.

Nennong, C. Randall and Martin Kessler (2012) "Fiscal Federalism: US History for Architects of Europe's Fiscal Union," Peterson Institute for International Economics, Working Paper 12-2.

Niskanen, W. A., Jr. (1971) *Bureaucracy and Representative Government* (Chicago:Aldine-Atherton).

Passarelli, Francesco and Guido Tabellini (2013) "Emotions and Political Unrest," CESifo Working Paper no. 4165 (March).

Peacock, Alan (1992), *Public Choice Analysis in Historical Perspective*, Mattioli Lectures (Cambridge University Press).

Phelps, E.S. (2010) "The Slump, the Recovery and the "New Normal," *Capitalism and Society*, **5** (2), art. 2.

Pisani-Ferry, Jean (2012) "The Euro Crisis and the New Impossible Trinity," Bruegel Policy Contribution (January).

Polackova Brixi, Hana and Allen Schick (eds) (2002) *Government at Risk: Contingent Liabilities and Fiscal Risk* (Washington, DC: World Bank, and Oxford University Press).

Poterba, James M. (1995) "Balanced Budget Rules and Fiscal Policy: Evidence from the States," *National Tax Journal*, **48** (3), 329–36.

Puddu, Stefano and Andreas Walchli (2012) "The Term Action Facility Effect on Liquidity Risk Exposure," *Vox* (12 December).

Ragazzi, Giorgio (ed.) (1997) *Trasparenza nei conti pubblici e controllo della spesa* (Milan: Franco Angeli).

Rajan, R. (2010) *Fault Lines* (Princeton University Press).

Reinhart, Carmen and Kenneth S. Rogoff (2009) *This Time is Different: Eight Centuries of Financial Folly* (Princeton University Press).

Reinhart, Carmen and Kenneth S. Rogoff (2011a) A *Decade of Debt*, Policy Analyses in International Economics 95 (Washington, DC: Peterson Institute for International Economics) (September).

Reinhart, Carmen and Kenneth S. Rogoff (2011b) "From Financial Crash to Debt Crisis," *American Economic Review*, **101** (5), 1676–1706.

Reviglio, Franco (2001) "Budgetary Transparency for Public Spending Control," in *International Journal of Public Budget*, **46** (July/August), year 28.

Sancak, C., R. Velloso, and J. Xing (2010) "Tax Revenue response to the Business Cycle," IMF Working Paper 10/71.

Schuknecht, Ludger and Vito Tanzi (2005) *Reforming Public Spending: Great Gain, Little Pain* (London: Politeia).

Schuknecht, Ludger and Vito Tanzi (2006) "Reforming Public Expenditure in Industrialized Countries: Public Spending and Social Welfare," in Peter Wierts, Servaas Deroose, Elena Flores, and Alessandro Turrini (eds), *Fiscal Policy Surveillance in Europe* (Basingstoke: Palgrave Macmillan).

Schuknecht, Ludger (2012) "Has Public Insurance Gone Too Far?," mimeo, December.

Seminerio, Mario (2012) *La cura letale* (Rome and Milan: Biblioteca Universale Rizzoli, BUR).

Sinn, Hans-Werner (2010) *Casino Capitalism* (Oxford University Press).
Sinn, Hans-Werner (ed.) (2012) "The European Balance of Payment Crisis," Special Issue of *CESifo Forum*, vol. 13 (January).
Sinn, Hans-Werner and Timo Wollmershäuser (2011) "Target Loans, Current Accounts Balances and Capital Flows: The ECB's Rescue Facility," CESifo Working Paper no. 3500 (24 June). Published in *International Tax and Public Finance,* **19** (4), 468–508.
Spilimbergo A., S. Symansky, O. Blanchard, and C. Cottarelli (2008) "Fiscal Policy for the Crisis," IMF Staff Position Note 08/01 (Washington, DC, 29 December).
Suskind, Ron (2011) *Confidence Men: Wall Street, Washington, and the Education of a President* (New York: HarperCollins).
Tanzi, Vito (1978) "Inflation, Real Tax Revenue and the Case for Inflationary Finance: Theory with an Application to Argentina," IMF Staff Papers, **25** (4), 623–49.
Tanzi, Vito (1980) "Inflationary Expectations, Economic Activity, Taxes, and Interest Rates," *American Economic Review,* **70** (1), 12–21.
Tanzi, Vito (1989) "International Coordination of Fiscal Policies: Current and Future Issues," in Mario Monti (ed.) *Fiscal Policy, Economic Adjustment, and Financial Markets* (Washington, DC: IMF, and Milan: Bocconi University).
Tanzi, Vito (1992) "Discussion on Market-Based Discipline in Monetary Unions," in, M. Canzoneri, V. Grilli, and P. Masson (eds), *Establishing a Central Bank: Issues in Europe and Lessons from the United States* (Cambridge University Press).
Tanzi, Vito (1995) *Taxation in an Integrating World* (Washingon, DC: Brookings Institution).
Tanzi, Vito (2001) "Globalization, Technological Developments and the Work of Fiscal Termites," *Brooklyn Journal of International Law*, **26** (4), 1261–84.
Tanzi, Vito (2004) "The Stability and Growth Pact: Its Role and Future," *Cato Journal*, **24** (1–2), 57–69.
Tanzi, Vito (2005) "The Economic Role of the State in the 21st Century", *Cato Journal,* **25** (3), 617–38; also published in *Materialy i Studia* by the National Bank of Poland (Warsaw).
Tanzi, Vito (2007a) *Argentina: An Economic Chronicle* (New York: Jorge Pinto Books).
Tanzi, Vito (2007b) "Fiscal Policy and Fiscal Rules in the European Union," in Anders Aslund and Marek Dabrowski (eds), *Europe After Enlargement* (Cambridge University Press).
Tanzi, Vito (2007c) "Complexity and Systemic Failure," in Saul Estrin, Grzegorz W. Kolodko, and Milica Uvalic (eds), *Transition and Beyond* (Basingstoke: Palgrave Macmillan).
Tanzi, Vito (2008a) "The Stability and Growth Pact and Its Revisions," in *A Europae os Desafios do Seculo XXI* (Almedina: Coimbra).
Tanzi, Vito (2008b) *Peoples, Places and Policies: China, Japan and Southeast Asia* (New York: Jorge Pinto Books).

Tanzi, Vito (2011a) *Government versus Markets: The Changing Economic Role of the State* (Cambridge University Press).
Tanzi, Vito (2011b) "The Return to Fiscal Rectitude after the Recent Escapade," *Rivista di Politica Economica*, 1911–2011, no. 100.
Tanzi, Vito (2011c) A *Century and a Half of Public Finances in Italy* (Turin: IBL Libri).
Tanzi, Vito (2012a) *Realistic Recovery: Why Keynesian Solutions Will Not Work* (London: Politeia).
Tanzi, Vito (2012b) "The Role of Fiscal Imbalances and their Consolidation," paper presented at the European Commission Forum on "Tax Policies Under a Common Currency" (Brussels, 5–6 March).
Tanzi, Vito (2012c) "Taxing the Big" (mimeo).
Tanzi, Vito and Ludger Schuknecht (2007) "Reconsidering the Fiscal Role of Government: an International Perspective," *American Economic Review*, May 1997.
Tanzi, Vito and Ludger Schuknecht (2000) *Public Spending in the 20th Century*, (Cambridge University Press).
Tanzi, Vito and Nigel Chalk (2000) "Impact of Large Public Debt on Growth in the EU: A Discussion of Potential Channels," ch. 2 of *Public Debt and Fiscal Policy in EMU, in European Economy, Reports and Studies* (Brussels: European Commission), pp. 23–43.
Tasker, Peter (2013) "Japanomics Goes Where Few Nations Have Gone Before," *Financial Times*, Comment and Analysis, 12–13 January, p. 7.
Tobin, James (1966) National Economic Policy: Essays (New Haven, CT: Yale University Press).
Torres, Craig and Bob Ivry (2011) "Dying Banks Kept Alive: Secret Fed Data will Reveal" *Bloomberg News*, 29 March.
Von Hagen, J. (1991) "A Note on the Empirical Effectiveness of Formal Fiscal Restraints," *Journal of Public Economics*, **44** (2), 199–210.
White, William R. (2012) "Ultra Easy Monetary Policy and the Law of Unintended Consequences," Federal Reserve Bank of Dallas, Globalization and Monetary Policy Institute, Working Paper no. 126.
Wildasin, David E. (2009) "Intergovernmental Transfers to Local Governments," IFIR Working Paper no. 2009–11.
Woodward, Bob (2005) *Maestro: Greenspan's Fed and the American Boom* (New York: Simon & Schuster).
Zoega, G. (2010) "The Financial Crisis: Joblessness and Investmentlessness," *Capitalism and Society*, 5 (2), art. 3.

# Index

Printed and bound in Great Britain by
CPI Group (UK) Ltd, Croydon, CR0 4YY